A Late Chrysanthemum

The first half of this century saw the coming of age of the Japanese short story. Influenced by Western literary techniques, such innovative writers as Shiga Naoya, Ozaki Shiro, Yasunari Kawabata, Shimaki Kensaku, Hayashi Fumiko, Dazai Osamu, and (somewhat later) Kobo Abé reassessed the Japanese story tradition and brought new vigor to the uniquely Japanese sense of the detail and natural context of everyday life.

The works of these writers stand at the center of modern Japan's literary development. Despite their differences, it is the simplicity and purity of their natural images—sultry late-summer days, cicadas, lizards, and the sounds of life's routines—that more than anything anchor the emotions and perceptions of their stories.

For *A Late Chrysanthemum*, translator and editor Lane Dunlop has selected twenty-one stories by these seven intriguing and influential authors to convey the depth and range of the modern Japanese story, a discriminating selection which, in Dunlop's sure and masterful English renderings, won this book the Japan-United States Friendship Award for Literary Translation.

A Late Chrysanthemum

Twenty-one Stories from the Japanese

TRANSLATED BY

Lane Dunlop

CHARLES E. TUTTLE COMPANY
Tokyo, Japan

Published by the Charles E. Tuttle Company, Inc.
of Rutland, Vermont & Tokyo, Japan
with editorial offices at
2-6 Suido 1-chome, Bunkyo-ku, Tokyo 112
by special arrangement with North Point Press, Berkeley, California

Grateful acknowledgment is extended to the authors' estates for grant-
ing permission to publish these English translations: "Akagaeru,"
"Mukade," "Kuroneko," and "Jigabachi" by Shimaki Kensaku copyright © Kyo Asakura, originally published in Japan, all rights reserved; "Kajika" and "Sekirei no Su" by Ozaki Shiro copyright ©
Kiyoko Ozaki, September 1927, originally published in Japan, all
rights reserved; "Kinosaki nite," "Kamisori," "Chijo," and "Hai iro
no Tsuki" by Shiga Naoya copyright © Shiga Naokichi, October 1917,
originally published in Japan, all rights reserved; "Bangiku" by Hayashi Fumiko copyright © Ryokubin Hayashi, November 1948, originally published in Japan, all rights reserved; "Omoide," "Chiyojo,"
"Ogon Fukei," and "Toro" by Dazai Osamu copyright © Michiko
Tsushima, March 1933, originally published in Japan, all rights reserved; "Suruga no Reijo," "Gumi Nusutto," and "Batta to Suzumu-
shi" by Kawabata Yasunari copyright © Mrs. Hideko Kawabata, originally published in Japan, all rights reserved; "Akai Mayu," "Kozui,"
and "Bo" by Abé Kobo copyright © Abé Kobo, originally published
in Japan, all rights reserved.

Translation and Translator's Notes copyright ©1986 by Lane Dunlop
First published in the English language by North Point Press

First Tuttle edition, 1988
Second printing, 1991

ISBN 0-8048-1578-X
Printed in Japan

Contents

Translator's Preface

The seven writers in this selection are significant writers, represented by some of their best-known work. Shiga Naoya, for instance, is known as "the god of the short story" for his dominant influence in the genre, and the two stories by the major novelist Ozaki Shiro are thought to be among his very best. And of how many writers can it be said, as of Dazai Osamu, that their graves are decorated every year on their death anniversaries by schoolgirls in a spontaneous outpouring of respectful affection? Kawabata of course needs no introduction, and the four stories of Shimaki Kensaku in this book, all written while he was in bed with his final illness, are regarded as the enduring kernel of his work.

Most of the stories are from what is generally agreed to be the golden age of twentieth-century Japanese literature, the *entre deux guerres* period from the close of the Russo-Japanese War (1905) to the onset of World War II, or "The Pacific War" as it's called in Japan. During this period, a necessary freshening Western influence was kept nicely in balance with what was unique to Japan. Western form was given Japanese content: the details of everyday living peculiar to Japan then, a feeling for Nature and a disposition to look there for clues as to how to live one's life, and a belief in purity and simplicity of feeling as their own justification. I would call particular attention to the awareness of Nature in many of these stories. Time and again, it is the natural detail that serves to set an experience in memory. "The dusky room on the bank of the Edogawa, the sultry late-summer day, came back to her. She could hear the steady, clunking sound of the automatic irrigation pump, the cicada's ascending cry." This is the memory of a love affair in Hayashi Fumiko's "A Late Chrysanthemum." Such awareness of Nature's presence, sometimes as unobtrusive as a phrase about the way the light looks at a certain hour, amounts to a saving grace.

These qualities, alas, have largely been lost in the postwar period. In the work of Kobo Abé, we emerge into the thoroughly alienated, urban-centered consciousness of international modern writing. Yet even so, in the Kafka-esque transmogrifications of his hapless characters, there is a sort of gentleness and vestigial love of Nature: they turn, not into gigantic cockroaches, but into a red cocoon, a stick, and a sort of water.

LANE DUNLOP

Acknowledgments

Acknowledgments are due to the editors of the following magazines, in which these stories first appeared in slightly different form: *Prairie Schooner* for "Infatuation," "A Gray Moon," "At Kinosaki," "The Grasshopper and the Bell Cricket," "The Silverberry Thief," "The Young Lady of Suruga," and "The Red Frog"; *New England Review/Bread Loaf Quarterly* for "The Razor" and "River Deer"; *Translation* for "The Wagtail's Nest" and "A Late Chrysanthemum"; *Antaeus* for "The Centipede"; *Stand* for "The Black Cat"; *The Missouri Review* for "The Wasps"; *Mississippi Review* for "Memories," "A Golden Picture," and "The Garden Lantern"; *Michigan Quarterly Review* for "Chiyojo"; *TriQuarterly* for "The Red Cocoon," "The Flood," and "The Stick."

A Late
Chrysanthemum

SHIGA NAOYA
[1883–1971]

Infatuation

It was a cold, thinly overcast day. With a slight headache from the chill and feeling much depressed, he'd shut himself up in his study. From time to time snow had been falling, hiding the mountains beyond. There was a pond in the garden, and the snow would quickly fall and disappear in it. As he looked through the panes of the shoji and the glass outer door, the snow stopped and blue sky appeared. It was typical mountain weather.

He could not make up his mind what to do in this affair. It would be best to give up the woman, but he disliked that idea as having come from his wife. The woman herself felt no affection for him. If he came to feel nothing for her and they quietly separated, well and good. But he could not steel himself to the forced obedience of leaving her now, although for a while he had meant to. Nevertheless it was disagreeable to go on deceiving his wife, who for her part had been magnanimous in the affair. If he added this to all the previous considerations, it was clearly an impossible situation. It would have been ideal, of course, had it been possible for *him*. He had even gone so far as to suggest the possibility the night before, but had immediately realized that it was a hopeless venture.

His wife had asked him to settle the affair today. She was in earnest. He could not compete with her sincerity. He had thought that he was being unusually serious himself but was far behind his wife in this respect.

At any rate, he had decided that a short, formal separation was the only answer. His wife's saying that it could be done with money, though, unpleasantly revealed her contempt for the woman. He could not easily stomach it. No doubt she spoke the truth, and he might have said the same of another person. But it was unlike his wife to say it. He understood that she spoke as one who had been betrayed and cheated, but it annoyed him nonetheless.

Even after he'd fallen in love with the woman, his feelings toward his wife had in no way changed. Rather, his wife had continued to derive a charm from the thought of the torment he inflicted by deceiving her. But now that things between them had come down to such a blank openness, even this gave him only a dry, chilled feeling. To have changed so suddenly—if only for a while—seemed the act of a coward.

The woman was a waitress in a Gion teahouse. A big-boned, mannish girl of twenty or so, she had no such spiritual problems. It was strange even to him how he could have been so attracted to her. Her beauty belonged to a type he liked, but it astonished him that he had been so deeply drawn to her.

There was a savor in this girl, long since lost in his wife, of a fresh fruit. Her breath was as fragrant as any child's. Her flesh was like the pure white meat of a crab caught in northern seas. So far as all these were the charms of a physical fascination, his was a vulgar emotion; and yet, in the passion by which he was endlessly drawn to her, beyond so-called dissipation, he could see nothing but love. Having its own beauty, even that which was ugly in her did not seem ugly to him.

His thoughts made him grimace to himself. Just then his wife, all the more excited for being overstimulated and tired, came into the room.

6

"Isn't it getting late for the bank?"

"Won't tomorrow do as well?"

"No. You must take care of it today. The longer it's put off the longer I suffer. I should never have let you think it was your own affair. It's past one. I have things to do myself. Please get ready now."

"You should stay indoors."

"No. I cannot sit at home."

"But don't you have a fever?"

"It would be nice if I got sick, wouldn't it? Got sick and died—isn't that what you really want?"

He glared up at her.

"Stop talking about things you don't understand—even as a joke."

" 'Things I don't understand'—is that how little it means to you?"

"It's not a question of life and death."

"I wonder."

"Only a fool would lump them together."

"That doesn't mean they *aren't* together."

He was aware that what she said as his wife could not invariably be dismissed as overstatement, and yet it angered him.

"Are you threatening me? It's vulgar to try and control people's actions that way."

His wife was silent. He'd spat out the venomous words just as they came to him.

Paling, his wife looked at him intently and then lowered her eyes. Sighing, she said:

"You really are selfish."

"I have always acted on my desires."

"Yes, I knew you always did as you pleased. But to completely deceive me with that as your excuse, and then to nonchalantly accuse me of coercion and vulgarity—how do you do it? You're shrewdly penetrating when you judge others, but for yourself the rules are quite different. Why do you think that is? People who scold their children for telling lies don't mind their own, it seems."

7

"If it were good to tell you the truth I would, always. If you could stand the truth I would always tell it to you."

"That's not what I heard before. Are you getting desperate for things to say?"

It was unbearably disagreeable. He did not want to go on.

"What you said then was good. You did tell me all the truth last night? You aren't hiding anything from me? Give me your firm promise that you will never do this kind of thing again—allow me at least to believe that. I will forget everything that has happened up to now. Please let me believe that much . . . Well?"

"I can't promise anything. Unexpected things have come up. I can't undertake for the future."

"In that case I can't go on living."

There was a note of hysteria in his wife's voice.

"What will you do, if you can't go on living?"

"I don't intend to kill myself, but it will come to the same thing. It can turn out no other way."

With his wife in this state, he would have to temporarily break with the woman. The thought irked him.

After an hour's ride, they got off in Kyoto at Higashiyama-sanjo. Large, abundant snowflakes were falling. It was a good feeling. The sun had been shining when they left Yamashina, and they hadn't brought umbrellas. Their heads and shoulders exposed to the snow, they stood cringing from the windblown flakes. The street whitened as they watched.

"I'll be back in an hour or so. You wait for me at our friend's house. We must be as calm as possible about this."

His wife silently looked into his eyes.

"It's cold—you should go there quickly. Are you warm enough?"

His wife nodded.

"So. Until then."

Leaving her, he decided to walk the short distance rather than take the crowded trolley. Crossing the narrow street, he went into a shop to buy cigarettes. When he came out his wife was still standing there,

8

her hair and breast covered with snow. Looking as if she were about to cry, she seemed to say something in a low voice. She had noticeably weakened in a single day. When he went up to her, she laid her head on his shoulder and, as if appealing to him, said:

"It's all right, isn't it?"

"Yes, of course. If you stay out in this snow you really will get sick."

His wife finally went back. Her small head, with its bound coiffure perched on top of the thick shawl, seemed quite drab and pathetic.

Entering the place where he and the woman always met, he found the madam sitting at an oblong brazier in the darkened tearoom. She got up slowly. "A heavy snowfall." There was something lazy and catlike about her.

"Something has come up. She'll be in shortly."

The woman came almost immediately. When he told her she looked puzzled and was silent. At last she said: "No, I can't." Congratulatory presents had been received from all the geishas—she could not do it on such short notice. Her reasons were clear. The woman seemed genuinely disconcerted because of them. She began to cry.

"You don't have to make an announcement, do you?"

"It would soon be known."

"Probably it would be best if I went away."

He had no confidence that if he stayed in Kyoto he would not come here. It really would be as well if he left, he thought. When he said so, the woman replied: "No, don't." She turned her dull, tear-stained face toward the window. Her expression was merely one of vague melancholy.

He took the woman's big, heavy body onto his knees. Her lips were brackish from her tears. He thought of the similarly salty taste of his wife's mouth the night before, and how unlike him it was to be involved with two such women.

After a while, paying the bill and giving the woman money, he left. Outside it was still snowing in flurries.

The friend's house was on the grounds of a large temple west from where they'd gotten off the trolley. As he went in by the back gate he met his wife coming out.

"It was awkward just sitting there talking," she said as if apologizing. She looked up at him. "It's all settled, then?"

"Yes." He nodded. The weakness of his acquiescence bothered him.

On the face of it, he supposed, everything was settled. But the problem of his feelings was far from resolved. When the woman had asked him to come once more before he went away, he'd given her a vague answer. For himself, he had not the slightest wish to leave her. Everything had been settled, as his wife said, and yet it had not. Instead of deceiving his wife, he was now deceiving himself. If he was not deceiving himself, by acting in this way he deceived his wife anew and the woman as well. He was reluctant to deal with the problem squarely if it meant wrecking his domestic arrangements. Besides, he didn't think it mattered that much. The woman had disliked him at first. Although she didn't dislike him now, he knew, without his wife telling him, that for her it was no more than a transaction. This attitude of hers was not pleasant for him, but in her world it was morality. Even supposing that she loved him, it would be impossible for her to leave such calculation entirely behind her.

Nevertheless, he could not keep her out of his head alone or in company. He could not bring himself to break with her until he had, in some sense, made his peace with her.

The rest of that day, he and his wife walked around the city. In the evening they went back to Yamashina. From that night on his wife was sick. It had been wrong for her to go out with a fever.

Although his wife's illness was merely a cold, it refused to clear up.

"I feel much better now that things have been taken care of."

He was perplexed when she spoke this way. His answers were meant to reassure her but their tone was not cheerful. It was not easy to be cheerful with his wife so anxious to believe him.

Once they had this conversation.

"It's after all like an illness in the family, one which will leave no trace. But it will mean a shorter life . . ."

"An illness, you say. That doesn't mean you won't catch it again," he replied, turning it off as a joke. He found it simpler to talk this way.

At any rate, he wanted to get away quickly. He did in fact have business in Tokyo, but his wife's illness lingered on strangely and he could not leave her so. More serious than the illness itself was his wife's nervous condition. She was always more or less in a state of febrile agitation. Her plain wedding ring, which usually seemed embedded in the plump flesh, now slid off easily when she lowered her hand.

The following is a letter he received from his wife not long after, when he was in Tokyo.

I am glad to hear you are well. Since you left it has snowed every day, and is bitterly cold. Are you looking after your neuralgia? I worry about you all—glad to hear you're in good spirits. I meant to thank you for the present but haven't had a chance to write. Thank you, very much. Please forgive me for being my usual weak-minded self when you left. It wasn't at all that I was depressed, but I was in bed and not feeling well. Just now I was crying by myself, and so began this letter. I mustn't bother him, I thought, and held off as long as I could. But it became too much for me, and here I am writing you these silly things. When I'm alone I think about it and the tears start to come. It's over and done with, I think, but I can't help myself. I just cannot feel cheerful about it. Please don't make me suffer like this ever again. The monkey died after all. Even now I can't bear the sadness of it. I truly believe you. It was because I did believe you that this has happened. It's bad for us to keep things from each other. I am merely expressing a selfish wish and it may offend you, but I beg of you— my suffering begs of you. You said that I mean something to you—it's disgraceful of me to feel so gloomy, but when I think of what happened I forget what you said. It makes me terribly sad. Thank you for your letter in which you explain everything. It set my heart at rest.

I imagine you every day hard at work on your writing. Please take good care of yourself—don't catch cold. If your neuralgia is even slightly worse you should go to the hot springs at Hakone for it. I'm glad you got the warm clothes I sent after you. Nothing in particular to report about our evenings here. The children are well. I've stopped crying so much. Sometimes when I'm depressed and get to thinking the tears still come. I'm trying as hard as I can to cheer myself up. You said that you love me, so whatever happens I won't be afraid. It's only my selfishness—if I weren't alone, my nerves wouldn't act up so. Please forgive me for not having considered your feelings, and writing only about myself. But just writing this trivial letter has made me feel better. My love to you all.

He'd gotten back from a walk and was reading this when a telegram came. PLEASE RETURN. His wife's loneliness, which she could not bear any longer, welled up powerfully in him. He thought it was good that she hadn't tried to bear it any longer. Although his business was not nearly finished, he decided to go back at once.

"Is she still sick, do you think?"

"No. It's because I've had another woman."

His mother did not answer. "I should go back right now."

He packed in twenty minutes, and was in time for the last express.

A Gray Moon

As I stood in the roofless corridor of Tokyo Station, the air was still but chilly. The light overcoat I was wearing was just warm enough. My two friends having taken the Ueno train which had come in first, I was waiting alone for the Shinagawa train.

From a thinly clouded sky, a gray moon shone weakly upon the fire ruins of Nihonbashi. Perhaps ten days old, the moon was low and somehow seemed close at hand. Although it was only eight-thirty, there were not many people about. The wide, deserted corridor seemed all the wider for its emptiness.

The headlights of the train appeared far in the distance. After a while, it came swiftly sliding into the station. It was not crowded, and I was able to get a seat across the aisle and near a door. On my right was a woman of about fifty, in baggy work trousers. On my left, a boy of sixteen or seventeen who seemed to be a factory worker sat with his back to me. He was sideways to the door, with his legs over the end of the seat where the armrest should have been. I had glanced at the boy's face when I'd gotten on. His eyes were closed, his jaw hung slackly open, and the upper part of his body was slowly swaying back and forth. Or rather, he was slumping forward, pulling himself up, and slumping forward again, repeating the same movement over and over. There was something unpleasant about such motions continued even in sleep. I left just enough space between the boy and myself so that I would not seem to be avoiding him.

At Yuraku-cho and Shimbashi, the train began to fill up. Several passengers seemed to be on their way back from food-hunting expeditions. A ruddy, round-faced man of twenty-five or -six lowered his outsize knapsack to the seat between me and the boy, then stood straddling it. Behind him a middle-aged man, also with a knapsack on his back, was being pushed off his feet by the press of people. Looking at the young man in front of him, he said:

"You don't mind if I put this down?" Not waiting for an answer, he began to slip the pack from his shoulders.

"Wait a minute." The young man turned around, as if to defend his own knapsack. "There isn't room for two."

"Oh. Excuse me." The man glanced up at the baggage rack, but there didn't seem to be room there either. Twisting his body in the cramped space, he worked the pack back onto his shoulders.

Apparently having a change of heart, the young man told him that if he wanted to he could rest his pack on the seat.

"It's all right. Mine isn't that heavy. It would only be in the way. I thought I'd set it down a while, but it doesn't matter." The older man nodded his thanks for the offer.

It made me feel good to have seen this. I thought to myself that people's feelings had truly changed from the way they had been.

At Hamamatsu-cho and then Shinagawa, some riders got off but more got on. Even among these new and more numerous passengers, the boy continued to fall forward and catch himself as before.

"Just take a look at the face on him," a man's voice said. The man was one of a group of four or five office workers. The others burst into laughter. From where I sat I could not see the boy's face. But the man had a funny way of speaking, and probably the boy did have an odd expression. An atmosphere of good humor began to prevail in the crowded car.

Just then, the round-faced man turned to the man behind him. Tapping his stomach with his forefinger, he said in a low voice:

"That boy's just this side of starvation."

Seeming somewhat surprised, the other man looked silently at the boy.

Even the men who had laughed now seemed to think that something might be wrong with the boy.

"Is he sick?" one asked.

"Drunk, more likely," another one said. But then someone else said:

"No, it's not that." Perhaps having sensed what it was, the men were suddenly quiet.

There was a tear in the shoulder of the boy's coarsely woven factory uniform. It had been patched from the inside with a scrap of towel-cloth. Beneath the visor of the army forage cap which he had on backwards, the boy's slender, dirty nape looked forlorn. He was no longer swaying back and forth. He was rubbing his cheek against a strip of paneling between the door and the window. Like a child, he had made the piece of wood into a person in his fatigue, and was trying to snuggle up to it.

"Hey." A big man standing in front of the boy placed his hand on his shoulder. "Where are you going?"

At first, the boy did not answer. When the question was repeated, he said in a dead-tired voice:

"I'm going to Ueno."

"No, you're not. You're headed in exactly the wrong direction. This train goes to Shibuya."

The boy got to his feet and started to look out the window. Abruptly, he lost his balance and was thrown lightly against me by the forward motion of the car. Caught unawares, I did something which I could not comprehend afterwards. Almost as if by a reflex action, I thrust the boy away from me with my shoulder. It was an act that was such a betrayal of what I really felt that I was shocked at myself. I was all the more sorry and ashamed because the resistance of the boy's body against mine had been extremely slight. My own weight was down to a hundred and ten in those days. But the boy must have weighed far less than that.

I tried saying from behind the boy:

"You should have changed at Tokyo Station. Where did you get on?"

"At Shibuya," the boy answered. He did not turn around. Someone else said:

"Well then, you're coming full circle."

Pressing his forehead to the window, the boy peered out at the darkness. Then, giving it up, he murmured so that I could hardly hear him:

"It makes no difference."

The boy's words, spoken only to himself, stayed with me long afterwards.

The passengers around him didn't concern themselves further with the boy. Probably they thought there was nothing they could do for him. I myself felt that as things were there was nothing I could do either. If I'd had some food with me, I might have given that to him for my own peace of mind. Money might have been no help to him even in the daytime. At nine o'clock at night, there was still less hope of his being able to buy any food.

With the same gloomy emotion, I got off at Shibuya.

This incident took place on October 16, 1945.

At Kinosaki

I was struck and thrown to the ground by a trolley car of the Yamanote line. To recuperate from my injury, I went by myself to a hot
springs inn at Kinosaki in Tajima. If the injury to my back should
develop into spinal tuberculosis, it might prove fatal. But I was told
by the doctor that that kind of thing was not at all likely. If nothing
happened in two or three years, I would not have anything to worry
about afterwards. In the meantime, I was told, it was important that
I take good care of myself. So I had come here. I intended to stay
more than three weeks—if I could stand it, for five weeks.

I was still not quite clear in my head. My forgetfulness became
acute. But my mood was calm as it had not been in recent years. I had
a nice, quiet feeling. It was the beginning of the rice harvest, and the
weather also was fine.

I was all alone. There was no one to talk to. I spent the day reading
and writing, or sat in a chair outside my room vaguely looking at the
mountains or the road, or else took walks. A good place for walking
was the road that went up from the town by slow degrees alongside a
small stream. There was a little pool at a bend in the stream around
the foot of the mountain where trout congregated. If you looked
more closely, you might discover big freshwater crabs with hairs on

their claws sitting as still as stones. I often walked on this road before supper. As I went up along the small, clear stream through the lonely autumn ravine in the chilly evening, my thoughts were often of unhappy things. They were lonely thoughts. But in them there was this nice quiet feeling. I often thought about my accident. An inch or two either way, I thought, and I would now be face up under the sod in the graveyard at Aoyama. With a pale, cold, stiff face, the cuts on it and on my back just as they were. The bodies of my grandfather and my mother would be by my side. And yet, there would no longer be any communication between us—such were the thoughts I had. Although they were lonely thoughts, they did not disquiet me all that much. Death would come sooner or later. Up until now, in my thoughts, I had pretty much assumed that it would be much later, in the far distant future. But now I felt that I truly did not know when it would come. In a book about the life of Lord Clive, which I read in middle school, it was written that Clive was encouraged by thinking to himself that there was something that had saved him from a likely death, had kept him alive for a work that he had to do. That was the way that I wanted to feel about my own brush with death. And I did have such a feeling. But in the end my heart was curiously quiescent. Something like an affection for death arose within me.

My room, being the only room on the second floor, was comparatively quiet. When I grew tired of reading and writing, I often went out to the chair on the veranda. Alongside me was the roof of the downstairs entryway. There was a wainscoting where it was joined to the house. Evidently there was a wasps' nest in that wainscot. Every day, as long as the weather held, the corpulent tiger-striped wasps were out hard at work from morning almost until nightfall. When they emerged, brushing the sides of the loosely joined planks of the paneling, the wasps would descend to the roof of the entryway for a while. There they would meticulously adjust their wings and antennae with their front and back legs. Then they would walk about a bit. All of a sudden, their slender wings stretched taut to either side, they lifted off with a resonant buzz. When they'd flown up like that, they suddenly shot away into the

18

distance. The flowers of the yatsude being in bloom just then, the wasps clustered about its shrubbery. When I was bored, I would often watch the comings and goings of the wasps from the veranda railing.

One morning, I spotted a wasp that had died on the roof of the entryway. Its legs tucked tightly under its stomach, its feelers were drooped untidily over its face. The other wasps were perfectly indifferent to it. Although they busily crawled around it on their way in and out of the nest, they showed no signs of being otherwise affected by it. Certainly the wasps, as they went indefatigably about their work, gave you an impression of the living creature. And the one wasp by their side, which morning, noon, and night was always in the same place whenever I looked, absolutely still, tumbled over on its face, just as surely gave the feeling of something that had died. It stayed that way for about three days. Looking at it gave me such a feeling of quietness. It was lonely. In the evening, when all the other wasps had gone inside the nest, it was lonely to see that one little corpse remaining outside on the cold roof tiles. But what a quiet feeling it was.

During the night, there was a heavy rainfall. In the morning, it was clear again. The leaves, the surface of the ground, and the roof were all washed beautifully clean. The wasp's body was no longer in its place. Already the wasps from the nest were energetically at work. Probably the dead wasp had been washed down through the eaves' gutter to the ground. With its legs shrivelled up and its feelers stuck to its face, covered with mud, it was probably lying still as a pebble somewhere. Until the next change in its surroundings that would move it occurred, the little corpse would most likely stay where it was. Or would it be dragged away by ants? Whatever, it was certainly quiet. It was quiet because a wasp that had been nothing but busy, busy had become absolutely still. I felt an intimacy in that stillness. A short while before, I had written a short story called "Han's Crime." From jealousy of an old premarital relationship between his wife and a man who was his friend, also driven by his own psychological pressures, a Chinese called Han had murdered his wife. As I had written the story, it was mainly about Han's feelings. Now, however, I thought of writing a story about the feelings of his wife. Murdered at the end, under the ground of the cemetery—I wanted to write about that quietness of hers.

I thought I would write "The Murdered Wife of Han." I did not write the story after all, but the need for it had arisen in me. It was a feeling that differed greatly from the thoughts of the hero of a long story that I'd been working on before. I was at a loss.

It was shortly after the wasp's body had been washed away, removed from my field of vision. One morning, thinking I'd go to Mount Higashi Park with its view of the Maruyama River and the Sea of Japan into which it emptied, I left the inn. From in front of a hot spring called Ichi-no-yu, a small stream flowed gently down the middle of the road and entered the Maruyama River. When I came to a certain place, the bridge and sides of the stream were lined with people. They were having a good time watching something in the brook. What they were looking at was a big rat that had been tossed into the water. Desperately swimming, the rat was trying to get away. The rat's neck had been pierced with a fish skewer about eight inches in length. Three inches or so of it stuck out behind the head, and three inches or so stuck out from the throat. The rat was trying to climb up on the stone embankment. Two or three children and a rickshawman of about forty were chucking stones at it. Their aim wasn't very good. With a clattering noise, the stones bounced back off the embankment. The onlookers were laughing loudly. The rat finally got a toehold between the stones of the embankment. But when it tried to climb up, the skewer immediately got in its way. And so it dropped back into the water. The rat was trying to rescue itself somehow. A human being could not understand the expression of its face, but it was clear from its actions that it was trying very hard. As if thinking that if it could just get away somewhere it would be safe, still transfixed by the long skewer, the rat began to swim out toward the middle of the stream. Having more fun than ever, the children and the rickshawman threw their stones. Two or three domestic ducks, which had been foraging for food in front of a laundry stone to the side, were startled by the flying stones and craned their necks, goggle-eyed. The stones hit the water with a swift plunking sound. The ducks, their necks still stretched out, with silly expressions of dismay and squawks of alarm, made their way upstream with busily paddling feet. I had no heart to watch the rat's last moments. The appearance of the rat as it fled for its life with all its strength, laboring under a fate that would end in death, remained strangely in my mind. I had a lonely, unpleasant feeling. That was the truth, I thought to myself. Before the quietness that I aspired toward, there was that terrible suffering. I might have an affection for the quietness after death, but until I achieved that death I would likely have a dreadful time of it. Creatures that did not know of suicide had to continue their efforts until they had finally done dying. If I were in a situation similar to the rat's, what would I do? Wouldn't I struggle, as the rat had done? I could not but think of the time of my accident, when I was close to death. I had tried to do everything that was possible. I had decided myself on the hospital. I had designated the way to go there. Thinking that if the doctor were out, it would be inconvenient if the preparations for surgery were not ready upon my arrival, I requested that somebody phone ahead. Afterwards, it had seemed strange even to me that in a half-conscious state my mind had worked well on the most important things. The question of whether the injury was fatal or not was literally a matter of life and death. Even so, I was almost completely unassailed by the fear of death. This also seemed strange to me. "Is it fatal or not? What did the doctor say?" I asked a friend who was standing by. "He says it's not a fatal injury," I was told. This answer cheered me up immediately. From excitement, I became extraordinarily happy. How would I have acted if I'd been told: "It's fatal"? I could not at all imagine myself in such a case. Probably I would have felt sad. But I had the feeling that I would not have been attacked by the fear with which one usually thinks of death. I had the feeling that even if I had been told I was dying, I would have thought all the more of doing something to save myself. Doubtless I would not have been so different in that from the rat. Trying to imagine how it would be if

I'd had my accident now, I thought that probably it would be much the same thing. Doubtless what I hoped for would have no very immediate effect on how it was for me. And either way was all right. It was all right with me whether my hopes influenced my condition or not. There was nothing I could do about it.

Some time after this incident, I slowly made my way up along the little stream from the town one evening. When I crossed the tracks in front of the tunnel of the Yamakage line, the road became narrow and steep. The stream also became steep, and swift. There were no houses at all around here. Thinking to myself that I would turn back, I kept walking "until that place up there," on and on, around bend after bend. Everything was pale and faint. The air was cold on my skin. Oddly, the quietness somehow made me nervous. There was a big mulberry tree by the roadside. On the far side of the tree, on a branch that stretched out over the road, a single leaf was fluttering the same way again and again. There was no wind, and aside from the stream everything was quiet. In the midst of all that silence and stillness, the one solitary leaf was continually and agitatedly a-flutter. It struck me as peculiar. I even felt slightly afraid. But I was also curious. Going down under the tree, I looked up at that leaf for a while. Then, the wind began to blow. And as it did so, the moving leaf became still. The cause was evident. I thought that somehow I could understand such things better now.

It was gradually growing dark. No matter how far I went, there was always another turning. I'll turn back here, I thought. Casually, I looked at the stream off to the side. On the slope of the far bank, on a flat rock, about half the size of a tatami mat, that stood out of the water, there was a small black creature. It was a water lizard. Still wet, it had a beautiful color. Its head lower, it faced the stream stilly from the slant rock. It did not move. The water that dripped from its body trickled about an inch down the dark dry stone. I squatted down at ease and watched it. I was not as averse to water lizards as I once had been. I felt some liking for ordinary lizards. The lizards known as "shrine guardians" I detested above all others. As for water lizards, I neither liked nor disliked them. About ten years earlier, at Ashi-no-Mizu-umi, I'd often watched the water lizards gather around the spout where the wastewater from the inn ran off. I often got the feeling that it would be unbearable to be a water lizard. I thought of such things as what I would do if I was reborn as a water lizard. Since at that time I had such thoughts when I saw the water lizards, I'd disliked looking at them. But now I no longer thought about such things. I thought I'd try to startle the water lizard and make him go into the water. I remembered the way they walked, clumsily swinging their bodies. Still squatting, I picked up a stone the size of a small ball that was by me and threw it. I wasn't particularly aiming at the lizard. I am so bad at taking aim and throwing something that even when I do my best I come nowhere near the mark. I never thought that I would hit the lizard. After a clunking sound, the stone fell into the stream. Simultaneously with the sound, the lizard seemed to have leapt sideways about four inches. Arching its tail, the lizard held it up high. I wondered what had happened. It did not occur to me at first that the stone had hit it. Quietly, of its own accord, the warped tail of the lizard came down. Squaring its elbows against the slope of the rock, the lizard, the toes of its forefeet braced in front of it curling inward, weakly tumbled forward. Its tail clung to the rock. It was motionless. The water lizard was dead. You've done a terrible thing, I thought. I had often killed insects and the like. But the fact that I had killed the lizard without at all meaning to pierced me with a strange unpleasantness. It was something I had done, of course, but it was absolutely fortuitous. For the lizard, it was a totally unexpected death. I squatted there for some time. With the feeling that it was me and the lizard now, I became as the lizard. I lived that feeling. I felt it was piteous, and at the same time I felt the loneliness of all life. By chance I had not died. By chance the lizard had died. With a lonely feeling, I came back down the road, which I could hardly see in front of my feet, toward the inn. Distantly, the lights at the edge of the town began to appear. What had become of the dead wasp? Probably later rains had buried it under the earth already. What had happened to that rat? Perhaps about this time, having been carried out to sea, its water-bloated corpse was being washed up on the beach together with some garbage. And I, who had not died, was walking along in this way. That was what I thought. I felt that it would not do for me not to be thankful. But in actual fact, no feeling of gratitude came welling up in me. Being alive and dying were not positive and negative poles. I had the feeling that there was not that much difference between them. It was quite dark by now. I merely felt that the distant lights were there. The sensation of walking separated from the sense of sight. It was very uncertain going. Only my mind went on willfully working. It drew me all the more into such a mood.

After staying for about three weeks, I left that place. Already more than three years have gone by since then. I did not come down with spinal tuberculosis. That much at least I was spared.

The Razor

Yoshisaburo, of the Tatsudoko in Azabu-Roppongi, a man almost never ill, took to his bed with a very bad cold. The Festival of the Autumn Equinox being close at hand, it was a very busy time for his barber shop. As he lay in bed, Yoshisaburo regretted having fired his two shop boys, Genko and Jidako, the month before.

In the past, although a year or two older, Yoshisaburo had been a shop boy along with them. The previous master, taken with his skill with a razor, had given him his only daughter in marriage and retired shortly after, handing the shop over to him.

Genko, who had secretly desired the girl, quit immediately. But the good-natured Jidako, changing his manner of address from "Yoshi-san" to "Boss," worked hard and well as before. The old master died about six months later, followed by his wife in another six months or so.

In anything to do with the use of a razor, Yoshisaburo was truly a master. A man with a strong temper, moreover, if he stroked the skin and it was the least bit rough, he was not satisfied until pinching up the stubble hairs one by one he'd shaved it absolutely smooth. In doing this he never chafed the skin. Customers claimed that when they'd been shaven by Yoshisaburo, their one-day growth was not the same. He was proud of the fact that in ten years he had never so much as inadvertently nicked a customer's face.

About two years after he'd left, Genko straggled back, asking for his old job. Yoshisaburo, out of friendship for a former workmate, had rehired the apologetic Genko. But during those two years, Genko had gone to the bad. He was prone to neglect his work. Inveigling Jidako to go with him, he messed around with a dubious woman in Kasumicho who seemed to know a whole slew of soldiers. In the end, egging on the foolish Jidako, he even got him to pilfer money from the shop. Feeling sorry for Jidako, Yoshisaburo had often admonished him. But when it came to theft, there was nothing more he could do. About a month ago, he had fired both of them.

Now, there was an extremely pale, lethargic man of twenty called Kanejiro, and Kinko, a boy of twelve or thirteen whose head was abnormally long from front to back. At busy times before holidays, these two were good for nothing at all. Lying fever-racked in bed, Yoshisaburo felt a solitary annoyance.

As it neared noon, customers came crowding in. The noisy clatter of the glass door as it slid open and shut, the dry sound of Kinko's high, loose-toothed clogs as he shuffled about grated on Yoshisaburo's irritated nerves.

The glass door slid open again.

"It's from Yamada of the Ryudo. The master is leaving on a trip tomorrow night, so please sharpen this razor. I'll come back for it this evening." It was a woman's voice.

"We're sort of busy today. Wouldn't tomorrow morning be all right?" Kanejiro's voice asked.

The woman seemed to hesitate a minute.

"Well, by then without fail, then." Saying this, she slid the glass door shut, then opening it right away added:

"Sorry to trouble you, but could you ask the boss to do it?"

"I don't know. The boss. . ." Kanejiro began. Interrupting him, Yoshisaburo shouted from his bed:

"Kané! I'll do it." His voice was sharp but husky. Not answering him, Kanejiro replied to the woman: "Very well." Closing the door, the woman seemed to go away.

"Damn." Muttering to himself, Yoshisaburo took out his arm, pallid and faintly stained from the blue-dyed underside of the quilt, and stared at it. But his body, weary from the fever, was as heavy as a firmly planted object. With drowsy eyes, he gazed at the sooty papier-mâché dog on the ceiling. Flies were clustered on the dog.

Without listening, he overheard the talk in the shop. Two or three soldiers, talking about such things as the quality of the small neighborhood restaurants and the foul taste of army chow, agreed that nonetheless when it got cool like this even that wasn't so bad. As he heard such talk, Yoshisaburo started to feel a little better. After a while, he languidly turned over on his side.

In the whitish, cloudy light of evening that came in at the kitchen door beyond the three-mat room, his wife O-Umé, the baby on her back, was getting supper ready. Savoring his lightened mood, he watched her.

"I'll do it now." Thinking this, he raised his heavy body on the bedding. But a dizzy spell forced him face down on his pillow for a while.

"Do you have to go?" Gently asking this, O-Umé, her wet hands dangling in front of her, came into the room.

Yoshisaburo meant to say no, but his voice didn't carry at all.

Pulling back the covers, O-Umé put the medicine bottles and the spit-pot to one side. Yoshisaburo tried again.

"It's not that," he managed to say. But his voice was so hoarse that O-Umé did not hear the words. His mood, which had begun to improve so slowly, turned sour again.

"Shall I hold you up from behind?" As if pitying him, O-Umé went around behind her husband.

"Bring me the leather strop and Yamada-san's razor." Yoshisaburo flung the words at her. O-Umé was silent a moment.

"Can you do it?"

"It's all right. Bring them."

27

". . . If you get up, you'll have to put on the sleeved coverlet."

"I told you it's all right and to bring them. Are you going to bring them now or not?" His voice was fairly low, but loaded with ill-humor. Pretending not to hear him, O-Umé got out the sleeved coverlet and put it on him from behind as he sat up tailor-style on the bedding. Lifting one hand onto his shoulder, Yoshisaburo grabbed the coverlet at the neck and tore it off himself.

Silently, O-Umé slid open the door of the half room and, stepping down into the dirt-floored entryway, brought back the strop and the razor. There being no place to hang the strop, she drove a bent nail into the housepost at Yoshisaburo's pillow.

Even at ordinary times, when he was in a bad mood Yoshisaburo was unable to strop a razor well. Now that his hands were shaking with fever, he could not at all sharpen it as he wished. O-Umé, who could not bear to watch him work himself into a rage, repeatedly said: "Why don't you let Kané do it?" But there was no answer. At last, though, Yoshisaburo's endurance gave out. After about fifteen minutes, as if both his will and strength were spent, he sank down on the bed again. Immediately sleepy, he dozed off.

At lamp-lighting time, Yamada's maid, saying she'd thought she'd try them again on the way back from her errands, took the razor with her.

O-Umé made up some rice gruel. She wanted to give it to Yoshisaburo before it got cold, but afraid that if she roused him from his exhausted sleep she would put him in a bad mood again, she held back. It got on toward eight o'clock. If she delayed too long, it would be past the time for his medicine. Forcing herself, she shook him awake. Yoshisaburo, not all that displeased, sat up and took some nourishment. Then, lying down, he fell asleep again at once.

A little before ten, Yoshisaburo was roused again for his medicine. This time, he lay drowsily awake, thinking of nothing in particular. His fever-hot breath, trapped by the edge of the quilt which he'd drawn up to his eyes, unpleasantly mantled his face. In the shop, too, it was dead quiet. Listlessly, he looked around him. On the housepost, the jet-black leather strop hung peacefully. The dim light of the lamp was tinged a disagreeable muddy reddish-yellow. In a corner, O-Umé, suckling the baby in bed, lay with her back bathed in the light. He felt as if the room itself were pulsating with fever.

"Boss . . . boss . . ." It was Kinko's timid voice, at the threshold from the entryway.

"Yes?" Yoshisaburo answered with his mouth muffled by the edge of the quilt. Whether his husky, suffocated-sounding voice was inaudible or not, Kinko again called: "Boss . . ."

"What is it?" This time his voice was sharp and clear.

"A razor has come again from Yamada-san."

"Another one?"

"No, the same one. He tried using it straightaway, but it didn't shave too well. He says it's all right if it's ready by tomorrow afternoon. He wants you to test it before sending it back."

"Is the maid there?"

"No, she's gone."

"Give it to me." Reaching his hand across the quilt, Yoshisaburo took the razor in its sheath from the respectfully prostrate Kinko.

"Your hands are unsteady with fever. Wouldn't it be better to give it to Yoshikawa-san in Kasumicho?"

Saying this, O-Umé drew her kimono together over her naked breasts and got up. Yoshisaburo, silently reaching out his hand, raised the wick of the lamp and taking the razor out of its sheath turned the blade over and over. Sitting by his pillow, O-Umé softly put her hand to his brow. With his free hand, Yoshisaburo brushed hers away as if it were a fly.

"Kinko!"

"Yes." Right at the edge of the bedding, Kinko answered.

"Bring the whetstone here."

"Yes."

When the whetstone was ready, Yoshisaburo sat up and with one knee folded began to hone the razor. Ten o'clock slowly chimed.

O-Umé, thinking it would do no good to say anything, sat by quietly.

After a while, having honed the razor, he laid it against the leather strop. He felt as if the stagnant atmosphere of the room had begun to stir a little with the solid, stroking sound. Controlling his trembling hands, Yoshisaburo rhythmically stropped the blade, but do what he might it did not go well at all. Before long, the bent nail that O-Umé had put in as a makeshift hook abruptly popped out. Springing back at him, the strop wrapped itself around the razor.

"Ah! Dangerous!" Crying out, O-Umé looked fearfully at Yoshisaburo's face. His eyebrows were quivering.

Unwinding the strop, Yoshisaburo threw it down on the floor. Razor in hand, he got to his feet and, in nothing but his nightclothes, started for the entryway.

"You shouldn't do that . . ."

Lifting a tearful voice, O-Umé held him back. But he did not listen. Without a word, he went down into the entryway. O-Umé followed after him.

There were no customers in the shop. Kinko was sitting vacantly in the chair in front of the mirror.

"Where's Kané-san?" O-Umé asked.

"He's out dangling after Tokiko," Kinko answered with a serious face.

"What? He went out saying that's what he was after?" O-Umé burst into laughter. But Yoshisaburo had the same grim, set face as before.

Tokiko was a strange young woman whose family, five or six doors down, had a sign in front that said *Military Supplies and Sundries*. She was said to be a graduate of a girls' school. At that shop, there were always one or two soldiers, students, or neighborhood youths lounging around.

"We're closing, so you can go," O-Umé told Kinko.

"It's still early." Without reason, Yoshisaburo opposed her. O-Umé was silent.

Yoshisaburo started in honing the razor. Once he was properly seated, it went much better.

Bringing a cotton-padded jacket, O-Umé, with soothing words as if to a child, coaxed Yoshisaburo to put his arms through. Then, as if at last feeling easy, she sat on the threshold and watched Yoshi-saburo's face as he honed away with all his might. Kinko, in the customer's chair by the window, hugging his knees, was shaving his hairless shins up and then down.

At this juncture, briskly opening the glass door, a short young man of twenty-two or -three entered. He was wearing a new *futako*-lined kimono with a waistband and low clogs whose thongs were as tight as they could be.

"I just need a once-over. I'm in a big hurry. Can you do me?" Saying this, he stopped abruptly in front of the mirror. Chewing his lower lip, he thrust out his jaw and rubbed it energetically with his fingertips. The young man's speech was that of the streets, but his accent was that of a youth from the country. From his knobbly fingers and his rugged, swarthy face, it was clear that during the day he worked at hard labor.

"Go get Kané-san. Quick." Motioning with her eyes, O-Umé ordered Kinko.

"I'll do it."

"Your hand isn't steady today. So . . ."

"I'll do it, I said." Yoshisaburo sharply cut her off.

"You're not yourself." O-Umé spoke in a low voice.

"My work-coat!"

"It's just a shave, after all. There won't be any hairs. Why not do it as you are?" O-Umé did not want him to take off the padded jacket.

Looking from the one to the other with a wondering face, the young man said:

"Is the boss sick?" As if flirting, he blinked his small, caved-in eyes.

"Yes, he has a slight cold . . ."

"They say there're some bad colds going around. You have to watch out."

"Thanks." Yoshisaburo spoke with bare courtesy.

When Yoshisaburo had tucked a white cloth around his neck, the young man said again: "I just need a once-over." Then, adding: "I'm in a hurry, you know what I mean?" he gave a little smirk. Silently, against the thick of his arm, back and forth, Yoshisaburo stroked the blade of the just-now-sharpened razor.

"I like to be there by ten- or eleven-thirty," the youth went on. He wanted Yoshisaburo to say something.

Immediately, there floated up to Yoshisaburo's eyes a dirty woman in some dinky brothel, with a voice you could hardly tell was a woman's or a man's. When he thought that this vulgar little man would be making tracks from here to such a place, scenes that made him want to vomit passed one after another through his weakened mind. Dipping the soap into the completely tepid hot water, he savagely slapped on the lather from the jaw up to the cheeks. Even now, the youth continued to throw himself coquettish glances in the mirror. Yoshisaburo felt like pouring a stream of abuse over him.

Stropping the razor once more—*kyun*, *kyun*—Yoshisaburo started to shave from the throat upward, but the blade just would not cut as he wanted it to. And his hand was trembling. What's more, when he'd been lying down it hadn't been that bad, but now that he was standing with his face downward, watery mucus at once began to drip from his nose. From time to time, he stopped shaving and wiped it with the back of his hand, but soon afterward the tip of his nose again began to itch and the mucus gathered into a drop all ready to fall.

From inside, there was the sound of the baby crying. O-Umé went back in to it.

Even while being shaved with a blade that didn't cut well, the young man had a placid look on his face. It didn't seem to hurt or tickle him. Such stolid lack of concern got on Yoshisaburo's nerves until he was in a fury. Although one of his own blades would have cut smoothly, he did not change to it. His feeling was that nothing mattered anymore. Even so, at some point he'd turned meticulous again. If a place was the least bit rough, he had to go over it. The more he went over it, the angrier he became. His body slowly grew weary. His mind, too, was weary. The fever seemed to have grown worse.

The young man, who at first had talked of this and that, afraid now of Yoshisaburo's bad humor, fell silent. By the time the razor was at his temples, he'd begun to doze off from the fatigue of his hard work during the day. Kinko, too, leaning back against the window, was catnapping. Even the voice of O-Umé, crooning to the baby, had stopped. It was dead quiet. The night, inside and outside the house, was as still as the grave. There was only the scraping sound of the razor.

His fretful, angry mood turned into a feeling of wanting to cry. His body and mind were utterly exhausted. He felt as if his eyes were melting from inside with the fever.

When he had shaved from the throat to the cheeks, the jaw, and the temples, there was one soft part of the throat that just would not go right. After all the trouble he'd taken, he felt like slashing it off, skin and all. As he looked at that face, with its coarse-grained skin, the oil collecting in each of the pores, he felt that way from his heart. The young man had fallen asleep. His head dropped way back, his mouth gaped open. His irregular, yellow teeth were revealed.

The exhausted Yoshisaburo could neither stand nor sit. He felt as if poison had been poured into each and every one of his joints. He wanted to throw it all away, to drop down on the ground and roll around. Enough! he thought to himself any number of times. But by force of habit, he kept at it.

. . . Just slightly, the blade caught. The young man's throat twitched jerkily. From the top of his head to the tip of his toes, something passed swiftly through Yoshisaburo. It took with it all his weariness and disgust.

The cut was quite small. He stood there, simply looking at it. At first, between the thin little flaps of skin, a milky white color; then a faint crimson, steadily dyeing the cut. Abruptly, blood welled up. He stared at it. The blood darkened and swelled into a globule. Reaching its maximum distension, the drop flattened and streaked down the throat. A sort of rough, raging emotion surged up in Yoshisaburo.

Yoshisaburo had never cut the face of a customer in his life. The emotion came upon him with extraordinary force. His breath grew

33

shallow and fast. It was as if he were being pulled body and soul into the cut. There was nothing he could do, now, to resist that feeling. Shifting the blade point downward, he plunged it deep into the throat. The blade was completely hidden. The young man did not even stir.

A moment later, the blood gushed out. Quickly, the young man's face turned the color of clay.

Almost in a faint, Yoshisaburo, as if falling, sat down in a chair alongside. His tension immediately went out of him, and his extreme fatigue came back. Dead tired, closing his eyes, he looked like a corpse. The night, too, was as still as a corpse. All movement was in abeyance. Everything was sunk in a deep sleep. Only the mirror, from three sides, coldly regarded this scene.

OZAKI SHIRO
[1897–1964]

The Wagtail's Nest

The wagtail had made her nest in the shadow of the rock by the side of the town road. It was at a height that you could reach with your hand even without standing on tiptoes, but apparently no one had noticed it up to now. That was the story that Segawa came along with one evening. His inn and Minasato's were about three-quarters of a mile apart. There was only the one road, so every time he came to visit Minasato he passed by the wagtail's nest. It was in a place not too far from Segawa's inn. Just this side of it, there was a small wayside image of Jizo, the guardian of children. It was pitch-dark along that part of the road. The sound of a mountain torrent, carving out the darkness of a grove whose treetops were underneath one's feet, echoed up like a voice groaning in despair. However, a little beyond the Jizo, the rock-face came parallel with the road and then abruptly leaned back. When you came to the very end of it, the lights from Segawa's inn were visible. The wagtail's nest was at that turning. Most often, their attention seized by the change of the distant view, people did not see what was right before their eyes at the bend. Therefore, although one could say it was foolhardy of the wagtail to have built her nest there on the rock-face along a public road, one could also say it was an intelligent method. Because a place near a road is certainly favorable for avoiding snakes, and the wagtail was bound to fear snakes more even than human beings.

Segawa was strangely agitated as he talked. It made him uneasy that a young woman from the brothel at the edge of town had been with him when he discovered the nest and had peered at it from behind him.

The next day, Minasato went out to see that nest. Although he looked closely at the rock-face along from the stone Jizo, he could not find the nest at all. As he stood there, stumped, with nothing better to do, he struck a match to light up a cigarette. When he did so, as if startled by the sound, with a whirring wingbeat a wagtail flew up out of a small cleft of the rock right under his eyes. Flustered, Minasato stepped back. Because surely he had seen, at the top of that cleft, a little nest built up of dead grasses and, timidly astir in it, the heads of three baby wagtails. All at once, Minasato was troubled by a faint impulse. Simply by reaching out his hand, Minasato could easily snatch one of the chicks. It was not that he wanted the baby bird. Only, the feeling that he could satisfy an urge to steal without being seen by anyone stirred him up. Furtively, Minasato looked behind him. There was no one in sight. As quick as thought, he put out his hand. At almost the same instant that he knew his heart was a-flutter, in the gentle warmth transmitted through his fingertips he felt the life of a virgin girl. With no time to think of what he had just done, Minasato, clutching the baby bird and keeping it inside his kimono in his right hand, walked back toward his inn. As he came to the bridge where the road ended and continued as a new road, he felt the slight warmth from the body of the baby bird slowly fade away. Most likely he had held it too hard in his kimono. When he stealthily opened his hand, the bird had already died. Minasato tossed the little corpse into the tall grasses that grew alongside the brook. That same day, Segawa came by in the afternoon. Minasato told him that he had gone that morning to see the wagtail's nest. But when he said that there had been only two baby birds, Segawa said no, that couldn't be so. When he had looked at it, there had surely been three. Saying this, he frowned.

"Maybe that woman from The House of the Waterfall [the name

of the brothel] wasn't all right. I'll take another look this evening. If there aren't three, I'll question her."

From a feeling of having successfully deceived some unseen person, Minasato's heart, for no good reason, grew cheerful. He felt in himself a man who'd managed to get past a certain danger. Except that, for a moment, he had indulged a certain desire, wasn't everything as it had been? Minasato felt no unease whatsoever in thinking of it this way.

"Because she may have done a terrible thing. Come to think of it, on my way here today the mother bird was flying all around the nest."

To these words of Segawa's, Minasato replied composedly:

"The wagtail should have built her nest where there were a few more passersby. Her mistake was in thinking that humans always behave better than snakes."

In the evening, as part of seeing Segawa back, Minasato went out to the wagtail's nest. The sun was setting behind clouds. From the evening haze, there was a dampness in the air. There was a feeling of fall in the sound of the water.

As they came near the place where the nest was, whether or not it was startled by their footfall, the wagtail hopped up on another, higher corner of the rock. Bouncing itself lightly like a ball, it eyed the two men uneasily. Going up to the nest, Segawa took a long look into it. Suddenly, he called out in a flurried voice:

"There's only one. Only one—although there must have been at least two before."

Minasato was shocked. When he thought of it, somebody must have come after him and stolen another one. Minasato suddenly became uneasy. Perhaps that other man had covertly observed him stealing the bird. —Even if I don't take it, somebody else will. What's more, that man took one, so there's nothing wrong with my taking one.— Perhaps that unknown man, by thinking that way, meant to put the blame on me for his taking one. For a moment Minasato was drawn toward a moral feeling. But he instantly and fiercely sprang back from it. —Nobody saw me. Of course nobody saw me then. I can't let myself be frightened by this kind of illusion.

Minasato, however, feeling the sad eyes of the mother wagtail behind him, after he'd parted at the turning from Segawa who would go back to his inn from there, walked along the darkening road. As he walked, he thought about a girl whom he'd gotten to know since coming to this town. An only child whose parents were dead, she lived with her grandparents in an old temple on the main thoroughfare not far from Minasato's inn. Minasato went to the temple every night to play chess with the grandfather. To tell the truth, it was the girl he had in mind rather than the game. She would be fifteen this year. Despite the fact that her body was still a child's, in the depth of her eyes, dormant, lay the coquetry of a mature woman. It was not yet a month since Minasato had begun going to the temple, but in that time the girl's body had shown an extraordinary development. Exactly as when one watches, in the rainy season, a loquat take on the color of ripeness day by day, Minasato felt a fresh hunger for the girl. When they were sitting around the hearth talking, there was a moment when Minasato, in a flicker of light from the dim bulb, caught the girl looking at him fixedly as if in fear. Her eyes came after him all through the night. The delicate parts of her body tortured his imagination. That girl is waiting for me to come to her, Minasato thought. In his mind's eye, he saw a fruit dangling above his head. If he were to go to take it, he would not even have to stand on tiptoes. It would be enough simply to reach out his hand. The opportunity to do so presented itself to him any number of times. But each time, strangely, Minasato felt himself shrink back. Meanwhile, the girl went on ripening.

It was not to be wondered at that the thought of the girl should suddenly cling to Minasato's fancies. His fantasies went on expanding at an extraordinary rate. Now, at this moment, I can do anything I want, he thought. There is no reason why I alone should feel a moral responsibility toward that girl. Why is that? Because even if I were to hesitate to take it, that ripe fruit is sure to be taken by someone else who happens to pass beneath it. This thought worked up Minasato's appetite. "All right. Tonight. Me." He repeated the words to himself, as if to make sure of his own decision. That night, according to plan, Minasato went to the girl. And as he casually, ever so casually, touched the girl's lips, he felt that the girl's life was nothing more than the wagtail chick's that he had grasped in his palm. But as the night wore on, and, parting from the girl, he returned to the inn, his feelings were oppressed by a certain unexpected thought. He drew in his mind the face of a man whom he did not know. And—that man took one, so there's nothing wrong with my taking one.— It was the face of a man who muttered that, Minasato said as he described it later to Segawa. It was because he felt that a subtle power that ruled the girl's fate had been very clearly illustrated.

Some days later, Minasato, seeing off Segawa with whom he'd been talking until late at night, went outside. The hour was late; there was a moon and the air was crystal clear. Walking along the winding town road, before they knew it the two men neared the rock-face where the stone image of Jizo stood. Until then, Minasato had forgotten about the nest of the wagtail. But when they came before that image of the guardian of children, for an instant something terribly cold slithered across Minasato's heart. A wild, unlucky idea floated up in his head. What if there wasn't a single baby wagtail left in the nest? Treading stealthily, Minasato approached the shadow of the rock. The nest was where it had been. In the nest, a single wagtail was crouched with wings outspread.

"These past two or three days, every time I've passed she's been squatting down in the nest. Maybe she thinks her baby will be taken from her and is on guard."

As Segawa spoke, peering over Minasato's shoulder from behind, the wagtail, as if suddenly frightened by something, flew up from the nest. Flitting across the road, it vanished into the darkness of the grove.

Before Minasato's eyes, illumined by the faint moonlight, was an empty nest. A corner of its piled-up dead grasses was starting to come apart. The nest, like a vacated house, was full of emptiness. In it, Minasato could not see so much as the head of one small bird.

"That's strange. There's not even one chick in it now?"

Reflecting the moonlight, Segawa's eyes gleamed weirdly. Minasato felt the muscles in his cheeks grow stiff and hard. A certain scene flickered through his agitated mind. Across from him, around the small sunken hearth, sat the grandfather and to one side the grandmother and the girl. When, in the flicker of the dull light bulb, he sought out and caught the girl's melancholy eyes, which burned with a certain desire, he suddenly grew uneasy.

That girl, in the near future, would no doubt be seduced by some other man and run away from the temple. The premonition of it came home to Minasato.

The kitchen of the old temple, desolate and dreary without the girl, appeared to him in his vision.

River Deer

For the Ogatas, who were staying in the detached wing of a hot springs inn by the river, it was a time of exhaustion. They had drained from each other's lives all that there was to be gotten from them. In loving, in hating, there was already no freshness or life left. It was as if they had fallen into identical traps. By the repeated, wearisome habit of putting each other off with minor emotions, of favoring each other with morsels of affection that were more like leavings, they barely managed to feel different from each other. It couldn't go on this way, thought Araki Ogata. It was not that either of them was bad. It was just that the marriage itself was unnatural. Aside from the physiological distinction that he was a man and she a woman, they shared exactly the same temperament.

One night, they had this sort of conversation in bed. First, Araki Ogata's wife shook him awake.

"You. Don't you feel that by living this way we're wearing each other out? All of a sudden it scares me. I've thought of something good. We'll separate completely. You will go off somewhere with another woman, and I'll be left behind. It'll put some life back in our lives. We *will* separate, won't we? It's the only decent course of action."

"That sounds like a good idea. Let's start right away, shall we? But I'm afraid I lack your imagination. I'm reluctant to act. Maybe you can fill me in on my role."

"Oh, you're so cold! You can lie there and say that kind of thing so calmly—I've become completely unnecessary to you. Could you just silently look on if I went away with another man?"

"Why not? You've always had your own way. Can you deny that I've become even more unnecessary to you than you have to me? Anyway, we can't go on playing these childish games with each other. Therefore—"

"Therefore what?"

"I've been thinking of the hard facts of the situation."

"The hard facts? You mean we really will separate—completely?"

"Maybe. I don't know for sure myself. What I do know is that I'm tired of this kind of life. I want to be alone. I want to get back to my own life. As it is, I'm taking you around everywhere with me like a shadow. It would be better if we were enemies. That way I could get rid of you. But we're not—we're friends and allies. Allies who are fed up to the teeth with each other. And these stale arguments we're always having—it's the same thing. You don't have to say what you don't mean. I'll be glad to leap into whatever new chains you have to offer. —People should never be afraid to make themselves miserable."

"My, quite a sermon. If you're so anxious to be unhappy, you can do it on your own. As if you've ever thought of anyone except yourself."

"I—? All right, I do think of myself. But can you say you don't think of yourself even more?"

"You're quite logical, aren't you? I have never once thought of us apart. But you have always drawn a clear line between yourself and myself. I know you're making your mind up to leave me. I feel very sorry for you. It's the end for us, isn't it?"

Araki Ogata could not take any more. He felt the calmness of his mind slowly grow deranged. His wife's voice began to ring in his ears like a challenge. The memories of his several years of married life passed in motley review. They were all muddy, unpleasant memories. For a moment, he seemed to himself a calculating, insincere, worthless man. It would be an act of sacrifice, the best thing he could do for her, if he left his wife. Yes, he would leave her. He would be truly alone. —He purposely turned his body away from his wife. A sea, which faced on a white sandy beach glittering in the sun, appeared in his mind. He imagined himself lying down on the second floor of an inn situated among the sand dunes. Alone, I will set out on a journey. As he thought this, a new road suddenly seemed to open out before him. But this was by no means the first time that he'd had such a fantasy. Invariably, after an argument with his wife, his thoughts followed the same course and came out at the same feeling. Lashed with a savage self-contempt, Ogata waited for his wife's next words. I must not be sentimental, he thought. But when he had set himself again to leap beyond the bounds of fantasy, his wife, who had crept up close behind him, began to cry. He felt a powerful impulse being lured to the surface.

"You, is it really the end for us? Is it really?"

The warmth of his wife's body pressed against his body. Two palms, like the suction-disks on the hands of river frogs, fastened themselves to his back. You fool, stay out of this! Ogata yelled silently at the impulse like a throb of pain that rose at his wife's touch. It was an important moment.

"Is it really the end? Is it?"

"Yes, it is."

"And we'll separate?"

"Yes."

But after saying this, he suddenly felt his heart grow thin and empty. Clinging to his back, his wife began to cry convulsively. Her weeping voice amplified in the void of his heart. It was drawing him backwards little by little.

"You just stay here. I'm going out for a short walk."

Abruptly, as if dodging her, Araki Ogata stood up from his wife. He thought he heard her say something behind him. As if closing his mind, he firmly slid shut the door of the veranda. It was a clear, starlit night. He went down to the water's edge along the grassy path behind the inn. In front of him, the current was divided in two by a big boulder in midstream. Drenched with spray, slime gleamed along the sides of the boulder in the dim darkness. Sitting on his heels, Ogata fixed his eyes on the boulder before him. From the white tip of one of the waves that dashed themselves intermittently against the boulder, something black leapt up onto the rock. Ogata watched it climb with difficulty toward the top.

One, two, three—as he followed the progress of the strange creatures that wetly threaded the slime upwards, Ogata realized that they were the singing frogs called "river deer." In the darkness, with their hands and feet that were like human hands and feet, they clung to the smooth rock-face for all the world like tiny naked human beings.

Just then, when one of the frogs crouched on a corner of the boulder, it faced toward the stream and began to sing in a beautiful voice. Whereupon another and another clear limpid singing voice came through the noise of the river from around the boulder. They sounded in Ogata's ears as if aroused by some curious urge. The chorus of voices awoke in Ogata's heart a fresh sexual desire. He thought of his wife sprawled out tiredly, without energy, on the bedding. A strange, not altogether pleasant emotion stirred in him. Flustered, he was about to stand up when from the far shore a swarm of singing voices unanimously rose up into the night. —The singing voices were coming nearer on the current. Clinging to an angle of the boulder, a frog clambered up with deft movements of its body. After it, another and another, as if tumbling over each other, made their way up with throats full of song. The first frog, approaching the frog that was there before, leapt onto its body from behind. Tightly holding the other around the waist, it let its legs hang loosely. The tone of its singing voice abruptly changed. In a moment, the two overlapped frogs were inching their way down the rock. Presently the male and female frogs, stuck fast to each other, passed before Ogata on their way downstream. The next couple appeared. One after another, coupled in the same way, pairs of frogs with just their two heads above the surface of the two streams went on disappearing into the darkness down the river. As he gazed at this never-ending procession of river deer, Araki Ogata's head began to swim. As if drunk, he sprawled out on the river beach and began in a low voice to sing. The sky, a sea in which the stars were adrift, spread out overhead. Ogata listened to hear the sound of his singing voice dying into the noise of the river waves. He felt himself now in the presence of something extraordinarily solemn and sublime. In his vision, he saw himself embracing his naked wife from behind, serenely borne on the current after the procession of river deer. They seemed to him like heavenly bodies.

YASUNARI KAWABATA
[1899–1972]

The Grasshopper and the Bell Cricket

Walking along the tile-roofed wall of the university, I turned aside and approached the upper school. Behind the white board fence of the school playground, from a dusky clump of bushes under the black cherry trees, an insect's voice could be heard. Walking more slowly and listening to that voice, and furthermore reluctant to part with it, I turned right so as not to leave the playground behind. When I turned to the left, the fence gave way to an embankment planted with orange trees. At the corner, I exclaimed with surprise. My eyes gleaming at what they saw up ahead, I hurried forward with short steps.

At the base of the embankment was a bobbing cluster of beautiful varicolored lanterns, such as one might see at a festival in a remote country village. Without going any farther, I knew that it was a group of children on an insect chase among the bushes of the embankment. There were about twenty lanterns. Not only were there crimson, pink, indigo, green, purple, and yellow lanterns, but one lantern glowed with five colors at once. There were even some little red store-bought lanterns. But most of the lanterns were beautiful square ones which the children had made themselves with love and care. The bobbing lanterns, the coming together of children on this lonely slope—surely it was a scene from a fairy tale?

One of the neighborhood children had heard an insect sing on this slope one night. Buying a red lantern, he had come back the next night to find the insect. The night after that, there was another child. This new child could not buy a lantern. Cutting out the back and front of a small carton and papering it, he placed a candle on the bottom and fastened a string to the top. The number of children grew to five, and then to seven. They learned how to color the paper that they stretched over the windows of the cutout cartons, and to draw pictures on it. Then these wise child-artists, cutting out round, three-cornered, and lozenge leaf shapes in the cartons, coloring each little window a different color, with circles and diamonds, red and green, made a single and whole decorative pattern. The child with the red lantern discarded it as a tasteless object that could be bought at a store. The child who had made his own lantern threw it away because the design was too simple. The pattern of light that one had had in hand the night before was unsatisfying the morning after. Each day, with cardboard, paper, brush, scissors, penknife, and glue, the children made new lanterns out of their hearts and minds. Look at my lantern! Be the most unusually beautiful! And each night, they had gone out on their insect hunts. These were the twenty children and their beautiful lanterns that I now saw before me.

Wide-eyed, I loitered near them. Not only did the square lanterns have old-fashioned patterns and flower shapes, but the names of the children who had made them were cut out in squared letters of the syllabary. Different from the painted-over red lanterns, others (made of thick cutout cardboard) had their designs drawn onto the paper windows, so that the candle's light seemed to emanate from the form and color of the design itself. The lanterns brought out the shadows of the bushes like dark light. The children crouched eagerly on the slope wherever they heard an insect's voice.

"Does anyone want a grasshopper?" A boy, who had been peering into a bush about thirty feet away from the other children, suddenly straightened up and shouted.

"Yes! Give it to me!" Six or seven children came running up. Crowding behind the boy who had found the grasshopper, they peered into the bush. Brushing away their outstretched hands and spreading out his arms, the boy stood as if guarding the bush where the insect was. Waving the lantern in his right hand, he called again to the other children.

"Does anyone want a grasshopper? A grasshopper!"

"I do! I do!" Four or five more children came running up. It seemed you could not catch a more precious insect than a grasshopper. The boy called out a third time.

"Doesn't anyone want a grasshopper?"

Two or three more children came over.

"Yes. I want it."

It was a girl, who just now had come up behind the boy who'd discovered the insect. Lightly turning his body, the boy gracefully bent forward. Shifting the lantern to his left hand, he reached his right hand into the bush.

"It's a grasshopper."

"Yes. I'd like to have it."

The boy quickly stood up. As if to say "Here!" he thrust out his fist that held the insect at the girl. She, slipping her left wrist under the string of her lantern, enclosed the boy's fist with both hands. The boy quietly opened his fist. The insect was transferred to between the girl's thumb and index finger.

"Oh! It's not a grasshopper. It's a bell cricket." The girl's eyes shone as she looked at the small brown insect.

"It's a bell cricket! It's a bell cricket!" The children echoed in an envious chorus.

"It's a bell cricket. It's a bell cricket."

Glancing with her bright intelligent eyes at the boy who had given her the cricket, the girl opened the little insect cage hanging at her side and released the cricket in it.

"It's a bell cricket."

"Oh, it's a bell cricket," the boy who'd captured it muttered. Holding up the insect cage close to his eyes, he looked inside it. By the light of his beautiful many-colored lantern, also held up at eye level, he glanced at the girl's face.

Oh, I thought. I felt slightly jealous of the boy, and sheepish. How silly of me not to have understood his actions until now! Then I caught my breath in surprise. Look! It was something on the girl's breast which neither the boy who had given her the cricket, nor she who had accepted it, nor the children who were looking at them noticed.

In the faint greenish light that fell on the girl's breast, wasn't the name "Fujio" clearly discernible? The boy's lantern, which he held up alongside the girl's insect cage, inscribed his name, cut out in the green papered aperture, onto her white cotton kimono. The girl's lantern, which dangled loosely from her wrist, did not project its pattern so clearly, but still one could make out, in a trembling patch of red on the boy's waist, the name "Kiyoko." This chance interplay of red and green—if it was chance or play—neither Fujio nor Kiyoko knew about.

Even if they remembered forever that Fujio had given her the cricket and that Kiyoko had accepted it, not even in dreams would Fujio ever know that his name had been written in green on Kiyoko's breast or that Kiyoko's name had been inscribed in red on his waist, nor would Kiyoko ever know that Fujio's name had been inscribed in green on her breast or that her own name had been written in red on Fujio's waist.

Fujio! Even when you have become a young man, laugh with pleasure at a girl's delight when, told that it's a grasshopper, she is given a bell cricket; laugh with affection at a girl's chagrin when, told that it's a bell cricket, she is given a grasshopper.

Even if you have the wit to look by yourself in a bush away from the other children, there are not many bell crickets in the world. Probably you will find a girl like a grasshopper whom you think is a bell cricket.

And finally, to your clouded, wounded heart, even a true bell cricket will seem like a grasshopper. Should that day come, when it seems to you that the world is only full of grasshoppers, I will think it a pity that you have no way to remember tonight's play of light, when your name was written in green by your beautiful lantern on a girl's breast.

The Silverberry Thief

The wind is rustling
It blows in autumn

On her way home from school, a young girl was singing on the mountain road. The lacquer tree was in its fall colors. On the second floor of the weathered little inn, the windows were wide open as if unacquainted with the fall wind. The shoulders of some laborers quietly gambling upstairs could be seen from the road.

The mailman, squatting on the veranda, was trying to fit his big toe back into his torn, rubber-soled work sock. He was waiting for the woman who had received a parcel to come back out again.

"It's that kimono, is it?"

"Yes, it is."

"I thought it was about time for you to get your fall clothes."

"Now, stop that. Looking as if you knew everything there was to know about me . . ."

The woman had changed into the new lined kimono which she had taken out of the oilpaper parcel. Seating herself on the floor of the veranda, she smoothed out the wrinkles in her lap.

"Well, that's because I read all the letters you get and all the letters you send."

"Do you think I would tell the truth in something like a letter? Not in this business."

"I'm not like you. I don't make it my business to tell lies."

"Are there any letters for me today?"

"No."

"Even letters without stamps?"

"No, I tell you."

"What are you giving me that look for? I've saved you a lot of money. When you get to be postmaster, you can make a regulation that love letters don't need stamps. But not now, you can't. Writing me those smarmy love letters like stale bean jam. Then delivering them without stamps because you're the mailman. Pay the fine. I want the price of those stamps. I'm short of pocket money."

"Don't talk so loud."

"As soon as you pay up."

"I can't get out of it, I guess."

The mailman took a silver coin from his pocket and tossed it down on the porch. Then, drawing his leather pouch toward him by its strap, he stood up and stretched.

One of the laborers came thudding down the stairs in his underwear. With a sharp expression, such as God might have, a sleeping God who was tired of all His human creation, he said:

"I heard a coin fall. Give it to me, sis. You borrowed fifty sen."

"I will not. It's my candy money."

Deftly retrieving the coin, the woman tucked it in her obi.

A child walked by, rolling a metal hoop that made a sound of autumn.

The daughter of the charcoal-burner was coming down the mountain with a sack of charcoal on her back. Like Momotaro returning from the subjugation of Devil Island in the fairy tale, she held a big branch of silverberries over her shoulder. The crimson berries were splendidly ripe, as if green leaves had grown on a branch of coral.

With her bag of charcoal and her bough of silverberries, she was going to the doctor's on a thank-you call.

"Is just charcoal enough?" When she had left the charcoal-burner's hut, she had asked her father who was sick in bed.

"Tell him you had nothing else to give."

"If it were charcoal that Father had burned, it would be all right. But I'm ashamed to give charcoal that I burned. Should I wait until Father is well again and burns some?"

"Get some persimmons on the mountain."

"I'll do that, then."

But before the girl could steal the persimmons, she came to a place where there were rice paddies. The vivid red of the silverberries on the raised ridge path blew the melancholy of having to steal away from her eyes. She reached her hand to a branch. It bent without breaking. With both arms, she drew the branch down to dangle from it. Suddenly, the big branch broke off from the trunk and dropped her on her backside.

Smiling and smiling, and popping silverberries into her mouth, the girl went on down to the village. Her tongue felt rough and puckery. Some schoolgirls were on their way home.

"Give me."

"Give me."

Smiling openly, the girl silently held out the coral-like branch. The five or six children each tore off a red cluster.

The girl entered the village. The woman was on the veranda of the little inn.

"Oh, how pretty. They're silverberries, aren't they? Where are you going with them?"

"To the doctor's."

"Was it your family that came here to send a mountain palanquin for the doctor, the other day? They're prettier than red bean candy. May I have one?"

The girl held out the branch of silverberries. When the branch was resting on the woman's lap, she took her hand away from it.

"Is it all right for me to have this?"

"Yes."

"The branch and all?"

"Yes."

The woman's new silk kimono had taken the girl by surprise. Blushing, she hurried away. Looking at the branch of silverberries that spread more than twice as wide as her lap, the woman was taken by surprise. She put a berry into her mouth. Its cool sourness made her think of her own village. Even her mother who had sent the kimono was not there now.

A child walked by, rolling a metal hoop that made a sound of autumn.

Taking the silver coin out of her obi from behind the branch of coralline berries, the woman wrapped it in a small paper packet and quietly sat waiting for the charcoal-burner's daughter to come back on her way home.

On her way home from school, a young girl was singing on the mountain road.

> The wind is rustling
> It blows in autumn

The Young Lady of Suruga

"Oh, how I wish we lived around Gotenba. It's an hour and a half."

The train had arrived at Gotenba Station. Raising both her knees like a grasshopper, the girl stamped on the floor of the passenger car. Her face glued to the window, she watched as her classmates childishly nodded farewell from the platform. She spoke as if she would like to shrug her shoulders in boredom.

At Gotenba, it suddenly gets lonely on the train. Those who have made a long trip on the local rather than the express train will know this. At seven or eight in the morning and at two or three in the afternoon, the train fills up with a bouquet of flowers. How bright and noisy it becomes with the crowd of girls that go to and from school on these trains! And how short that lively time is. At the next stop, only ten minutes away, fifty girls have become none at all. Yet on my train trips, I have had such diverse impressions of so many girls of different places.

However, this time I was not on a long trip. I was going from Izu to Tokyo. At that time I was living in the mountains of Izu. From Izu, you change at Mishima for the Tokkaido Line. On my train there was always this time of flowers. The girls were students from the girls' schools of Mishima and Numazu. I went up to Tokyo once or twice a month, and in the course of a year and a half had gotten to know about twenty girls by sight. I remembered the feelings of the time when I had gone to middle school on the train. I ended by learning generally what car of the train those girls would be in.

This time also I was in the second car from the back. When the girl had said, "It's an hour and a half," she had meant from Numazu to Suruga. She was a young lady of Suruga. If you're a person who has gone beyond Hakone on the train, you probably know it. Suruga is a town where the girl workers in the big spinning mill across the mountain river wave white kerchiefs at the train from the factory windows and grounds. This girl was probably the daughter of an engineer or technician employed by the silk company. She usually rode in the second car from the back. She was the most beautiful and high-spirited of them all.

It was an hour and a half on the train, coming and going, twice a day. It must have been so long for her that her young doe's body grew stale and restless. Furthermore it was winter, so that she had to leave the house while it was still dark, and return after it had gotten dark. The train arrived at Suruga at 5:18. But for me, that hour and a half was all too short. It was too short to watch vaguely without looking at her as she chattered away, took a schoolbook out of her bag, did knitting, or teased her friends in the other seats. When we got to Gotenba, there was not much more than twenty minutes left.

Like her, I watched the schoolgirls walking on the rainy platform until they were out of sight. It being December, the station lights were already gleaming moistly in the dusk. On the distant dark mountains, the flames of a forest fire floated up vividly.

With a solemnity totally unlike her liveliness until then, the girl started to talk in whispers to a friend. She was graduating next March. She was entering a women's college in Tokyo. That was evidently what they were talking about.

We came to Suruga. From now on there would not be one school-girl on the train. The rain drove against the window my face was pressed against as I watched her go.

"Oh, Miss!" Wasn't there another girl who had run up to her when she got off, and hugged her hard?

"Oh!"

"I waited for you. I could have gone up on the two o'clock train. But I wanted to see you before I went . . ."

Under an umbrella, forgetting the rain, their cheeks almost touching, the two girls chatted busily. The train whistle blew. Hurriedly boarding the train, the other girl stuck her head out a window.

"When I go to Tokyo, we can see each other. Please come to my school dormitory."

"I can't come."

"Oh! Why can't you?"

The two put on separate, sad faces. The second girl must have been a worker at the spinning mill. She was leaving the company and going to Tokyo, but had waited nearly three hours to meet this schoolgirl.

"Let's meet in the city, then."

"Yes."

"Good-bye."

"Good-bye."

The factory girl's shoulders were soaking wet from the rain. Probably the schoolgirl's were too.

SHIMAKI KENSAKU

[1903–1945]

The Red Frog

A little before I was laid up I went to Shuzenji. At that point I was already near collapse, but did not think myself that I was gravely ill. I thought that if I gave myself a little rest I would soon be well. But the hot springs merely helped forward a passive disease such as mine. All I wanted was to be by myself in a quiet place. I had been to Shuzenji once before. It was not that I thought it a particularly good place, but other inns I'd applied to had written saying they were full up. And so I'd decided on Shuzenji.

I was disappointed from the moment I arrived at the inn. I had to regret having come. I was shown to a truly ugly room at the end of the corridor on the third floor. There was no fear of my getting too much sun—when I'd closed the door, I could hardly read the pocket editions I'd brought with me even during the brightest hours of the day. It was only midautumn, but the mountain air chilled me to the bone. Evidently I had a slight fever, for whenever a draft touched me around the neck I shuddered. Moreover, because of the draft, the smell of the privy was intolerable. Probably it would have offended others as well, but as my health deteriorated I became completely unable to tolerate odors of any kind—bad ones, of course,

65

but also fragrant scents. And so, closing the door, I would spend the day secluded in my dim room.

Occasionally I would get up and, sliding open the door, gaze enviously at the bright, sun-facing rooms across the way. I looked at the guests, lying full length in deck chairs on the spacious veranda. I could not think there was any great concourse of visitors, nor had I suddenly arrived without having made a reservation. Calling the maid, I tried to have my room changed but got nowhere.

At an inn of this kind a solitary transient like myself was the least desired type of guest. There were several good rooms empty, but they were available only for those who came with women. I remembered an incident that spring. I'd been touring the rural areas of Fukushima Prefecture on behalf of my radio station. I was taken by some locals to a hot springs place. After I'd removed my shoes and gone inside, they realized that I was alone. I was told there were no rooms and chased out as if with a broom. People who'd gotten rich off the military were everywhere. Such activities as quietly reading a book or resting one's weary body and wounded mind were beneath their notice. On the other hand there was the trade journal of the Hot Springs Association, with such statements as: "We of the hot springs industry, cognizant of our role as guardians of the national health, will comply with the New Structure . . . ," which had reached even this place.

I had expressly told myself that I would not get angry over trifles, that it was a defect in me to do so, and that there was nothing here to lacerate my spirit with rage. But the anger would flare up despite myself. Here too my illness was instrumental. When I thought of how I had worked myself to the bone making time, looking forward to this with pleasure, the mere sight of the books I'd brought with me to read incensed me. Transcending bad humor, I writhed in thoughts which are well described as venomous. I had no appetite whatsoever. At mealtimes an expressionless, unsociable woman would silently enter my room with a board on which were listed various dishes. Silently also and without reading it, I would place the tip of my finger by this or that item.

I even lacked the energy to try and find another inn, or leave this one and go home.

I came increasingly to spend my time away from the inn, only taking meals there. I went to such places as the hill, park, and plum orchard that mark the grave of Noriyori.* There I would pass vague hours squatting in the sun.

One day, I walked upstream along the Katsura River. I'd gone a good ways and turned back when I felt tired and wanted to sit down. I spotted a big roadside rock that directly overlooked the river. It was the size of half a tatami mat and perfectly flat. Seating myself on it, I wiped the sweat from my forehead. It was a bright autumn afternoon, with no one in sight. With a sensation of vagueness, as if I were having a light attack of anemia, I looked down at the water. At precisely the same distance from either bank there was a short, narrow sandbar. The stream soon met around it and flowed on as before. On my side it was deep, and small pools were formed by boulders that the current dashed against whitely. I could not see the bottom. Close in to the other bank it was shallow, and the stone streambed was like smooth wooden planking. The water raced over it noiselessly.

As I was vaguely looking, something caught my eye on the sandbar. At first I did not think it was even a lump of earth, but when it began to move sluggishly I realized it was a living creature. When I looked more closely, it was a red frog. Even for a red frog it was large, more like a toad. Perhaps it had been drying itself in the sun. But its reddish-brown coloring was rather vivid, as if its back was still wet. Lifting its hind parts, it slowly made its way toward the stream on the far side. The red frog reached the edge of the sandbar. There it stopped for a rest, as I thought. Then, with just a splash, it leapt into the shallow yet headlong stream.

"With just a splash"—it was a suitable way of describing its leap. Its legs were long and strong-looking. Sprung from the ground or through the air with a speed too quick for the eye, it was well into the

*A late Heian military figure. (tr. note)

stream while the taut line of its trajectory lingered on the retina. It was at a far remove from the heavy thighs, the sluggish dull feeling of a moment before. It was as if I'd awakened, as if a gust of fresh air had blown away not only the anemic mood of fatigue from my long walk, but my depression of the past few days.

The red frog was swimming with all its strength. It was trying to reach the far shore. The stream was not wide, but as I've said before it was swift. Stemming it, the red frog thrust its head forward. When it got to about midstream, where the force of the current was greatest, it was suddenly swept away. Seeming to struggle some-what, it was carried out of sight by the waves. Startled, I stared after it. Soon it bobbed to the surface in an unexpected place. Barely holding on to the extreme tip of the bar where it went underwater again, it clambered onto it.

There it rested itself. It seemed to me that its big stomach was throbbing as it fought for breath. Rising and falling, rising and falling, the red frog went forward again. When it came to the place where I had first seen it, it crouched stilly.

I watched it for a long time, somehow expecting something. Or it seemed long to me—probably it was less than five minutes. The red frog began to move again. As before, it reached the edge of the stream. Then it leapt, again as before. Swimming with all its strength, swept away, disappearing under the waves, clinging to the tip of the sandbar, crawling onto it, coming to the same place, and crouching—in every detail it repeated itself. With the feeling that I'd beheld some strange phenomenon, I kept watching it. Before my eyes, the red frog made for the stream again.

I remembered that when I first saw the red frog its russet back had gleamed as if wet. I had not seen this from the beginning, then. Before I saw it the red frog had repeated this performance I could not tell how often.

I burst out laughing. "You stupid frog."

The red frog wanted to reach the far shore. But there was no need for it to choose that part of the stream where it had just tried to cross. The stream there was rapid because of the smooth stone bed, but up a little ways it was leisurely and slow. There was a place where the current slackened and deepened a while, in preparation for the swift shallows ahead. Over that little pool, a big willow drooped its branches. It was an ideal spot for the red frog. Why didn't it try to cross there?

Even as I was thinking this, the red frog, having failed again, was making its way back. I was starting to get bored with it. Picking up some stones from the road, I began throwing them at the sandbar. I was not trying to hit the red frog, but to startle it so it would look around and take note of its surroundings. Several of the stones fell near it, others in the swift stream. Others fell plop into the pool, as if to say, "Look over here!" The red frog would cock its head and freeze an instant as if in fear, but in the end it went forward as before, leapt, and swam.

I stopped throwing stones and sat down again on the rock.

Unnoticed, the autumn sun had disappeared from view. The shadows of mountain and forest were already deepening. I had to get back before it turned chilly. But I could not bring myself to leave.

Gradually a strange idea took possession of me. It was that the red frog knew exactly what it was doing. I could only think that a will, a tenacious purpose, was at work in it. It was not that this small creature, gifted with a subtle life instinct, did not know where it would be easy to cross. I could only think that the red frog, with a certain purpose and the will for it, was boldly plunging into trouble. I could only think that having taken on a task beyond its powers it was struggling to master it. Perhaps, I considered, something lived at the bottom of that small pool that would swallow at a gulp the red frog swimming across there, or a snake lurked in the willow's shade that would dart down to make a mouthful of it. But it was natural for me to dispense with such possibilities, to go on thinking as I had been. It fitted in so exactly with my feelings.

The red frog went on doing the same things it had been. At first I'd amused myself by counting, this is the sixth, this is the seventh time, but soon gave even that up. From the time that the sunlight began to withdraw from the river's surface, the frog's actions had acquired a certain desperation. The intervals of rest before beginning again grew shorter and shorter. Once for a second I thought it had caught hold on the far bank, but it was washed away just the same. That may have been the supreme effort in which it squandered and exhausted its energy. Afterwards it seemed perceptibly weaker, and was easily repulsed by the current. Its strength appeared to be steadily diminishing.

The wind had begun to blow cold. Resignedly, I stood up to leave. A green frog could have made it, but there was no hope for this red frog. . . I brushed myself off. Then, one last time, I looked down at the river.

Despite myself, my eyes opened wide with surprise. In those few moments the red frog had vanished. I looked for it to reappear clinging to the tip of the sandbar, but this time it did not. I could not believe that it had finally gotten across. With a feeling akin to regret, I scanned the river repeatedly. After a while I started back, keeping close in to it.

Before I had gone thirty feet, however, I saw the red frog again where I did not expect to. This time it was directly beneath me, in close to the shore. The water was deep, and there were many boulders. The impetus of the churning, foaming current formed whirlpools or lashed it between rock and rock. The red frog was floating on one of the sheltered depths behind such rocks. It was perfectly clear what had happened. Each time the frog had been swept away it had latched on to the sandbar. Its strength failing, it had been unable to recover this toehold. Where it met beyond the sandbar the stream became broad and powerful. Engulfing the red frog, it had hurled it over against this side. For the red frog, it was a miserable state of affairs. Completely the plaything of the threshing waves, it had barely managed to stay afloat. Its present desperate circumstances were clear from the fact that near where it drifted behind the rock, a whirlpool exerted a steady pull on it. There was one means of escape left to it, and that was to climb up on the rock. But the rock's face was nearly vertical, and covered with smooth, gleaming slime. Its long back legs could not exercise their power in the water, and helplessly flexed or trailed behind it. Now and then its forefeet would catch in a little depression. It would flip right over, though, and I saw the red spots on the yellow belly as it floundered about. I wanted to reach a long stick to it, but there was nothing like that around me. So I simply watched to see what would happen.

Soon, facing the cavity in the rock, the red frog made what was evidently its last try to leap up. When it had turned over it remained that way, yellow belly upward, and without the slightest resistance, but rather as if quietly, peacefully going off, was swallowed up by the whirlpool. I hurried along the stream with little steps. I looked intently at the places where the red frog might reappear, but this time there was no coming up for it.

I felt a quietness, as if the scene had suddenly lost its life. And in fact it was rapidly growing dark. While walking, I went on thinking of what I had seen. The fate of the red frog, which after enacting its mysterious struggle had been pulled under exhausted by the waves of an autumn evening, seemed tragic rather than amusing. What tenacity of desire had driven it to this? I did not understand. I did not expect to understand. But I could only think that something more than the instinctive life of impulses was involved. The appearance of the red frog as it crouched stilly before going into action, as it flung itself into the swift stream and as it clung to the tip of the sandbar, as it got its breath—in all of this there was an expression, a mentality. It had been communicated to me as vividly as in the case of a human being. I could not have felt as I had if the frog had not acted from a definite will and purpose. How much more was this true of its last moments when it went under? It was like a warrior, sword broken, arrows spent, who had fought as hard as he could and at the end quietly obeyed his fate. There was a stillness in which these things were implicit. This was not a creature that had shared in human life like a horse or dog or cat. It was a frog. The fact that even from a frog this feeling had come moved me very much.

Perhaps some biologist could provide me with an unexpectedly simple explanation. A common explanation, based on the life necessities of a red frog. Perhaps his explanation would resemble the exposure of a fraud. Probably he would laugh at my stupidity in thinking that the challenge to a difficulty beyond its powers was itself of the will and purpose of the red frog. However I am not bound to agree with him. The biologist's explanation is well and good. But the fact that I received such a deep emotion from a small creature like a frog, the feeling itself cannot, I think, be explained by some learned analysis.

I felt deeply the mystery of the natural world as I had not for a long time. It was rare that even people like me raised their thoughts to the heavenly bodies, the universe, and made them a standard. Perhaps that was a kind of evasion. But a sudden disposition of the heart, as if I'd been saved, has remained with me. I am not the same person I was then. But common to both of us is a tense, stern reverence when we consider the mystery of nature, and yet a gathered trust from our awareness of a vast invisible will.

I went back to the inn with feelings completely different from those I'd come out with. Even my dark, cold, smelly room and the unfriendly people no longer bothered me at all. For a while I was even able to forget vulgar human life and society.

I left the next day. I had not read one of the books I'd brought with me. Only the image of the red frog stayed deep in my memory.

Even after my illness confined me to bed, I saw the red frog in my dreams. My dreams are almost never in color. But the yellow stomach and crimson speckles of the red frog as it went under were marvelously clear.

The Centipede

Late one night I awoke to a rustling noise by my pillow. It may have been the noise that waked me. Everyone in our house had grown sensitive to noises in the rooms these summer evenings. Perhaps because there was a cliff right behind the house, there were many centipedes. These centipedes had been completely unknown in Tokyo. Just a few days ago, one had crawled into my wife's bed. Even with the mosquito netting you could not rest easy. A little before that, my mother had been bitten. Taken by surprise, she had nothing by her to use as a swatter. With an old person's nonchalance, and faith in the toughness of her palm that could hold a fragment of glowing ember painlessly, my mother slapped at the centipede with her bare hand. My mother is from up north and knows nothing about centipedes. Probably she thought it was a kind of hairy caterpillar. But she learned what it was like to be bitten by one. Squeezing the bitten finger with her other hand, she screwed up her eyes and held her breath. It was both pitiful and funny. We had no ammonia in the house, and it being late at night we couldn't get any.

This sound was different, I thought, from that of a centipede dropping from the ceiling onto the tatami. It lacked that dry, rough, creepy feeling of many feet on the move. As part of my "fresh air" treatment, I slept with the windows open all night. Our house was in that section of Kamakura called "the valley." In the evening, when one turned on the lights, the swarms of insects were something to behold. We could not have stayed there without mosquito nets. An entomologist friend of mine once came to visit me. Peering out at the mountain that rose sheer behind the house, he said:

"You must have a lot of insects here. All sorts of unusual ones. You could just sit here, and they'd fly right into you. Why don't I give you some gear, and when you're feeling better you can collect a few."

My sickness cut me off from people and the world. My liveliest consolation was the evening dance of the insects. From inside the netting, I passed the time vaguely looking at them. When I turned off the light, the darkness came alive with a thousand tiny noises. The noises slowly died away, until only mute cicadas and Japanese beetles clung to the netting. Feeling relaxed and thankful that another day was over, I would fall asleep.

"Kasa, kasa, kasa, kasa."

I thought this noise might be one of the Japanese beetles. A frantic rustling, it reminded me of the little crabs I had played with as a child. It was from outside the netting but right by my pillow, from the washbasin. The washbasin had been placed there for when I brought up blood at night. I reached out my hand and turned on the lamp from inside the curtain.

It was no Japanese beetle that had fallen into the washbasin. It was an enormous centipede.

I called out loudly to my wife in the next room. She could tell by my voice that it was some kind of big insect. When she came in she had something to hit it with.

"Where is it?" The centipede continued its desperate activity.

My wife seemed to make up her mind to hit it as it crawled out. That was my idea too. I watched attentively. Then we saw a strange thing. Pointing its long antennae straight ahead, the centipede repeatedly circled the inside of the small bowl. But it did not try to get out. It could not get out.

74

I burst out laughing. "Completely helpless!" Somewhat more at ease, I decided to observe it a while.

The washbasin was enamelled all over. Circling at the bottom, the centipede presently raised its head and began climbing to the top. It managed to ascend to where it was just under the rim. But there, because of the concave sides of the bowl, half the centipede's body was floating in air. Its many legs worked busily and in vain. The very number of the legs multiplied one's sense of wasted effort. It was a ridiculous sight. The centipede hung on grimly to its laboriously achieved toehold. Its strength giving out, it slid back down. This scene was repeated over and over again. The slippery enamel surface was extremely unsuited to the centipede. Even at the bottom, its progress was awkward and slow.

We watched as it did the same thing ten or more times. Evidently thinking she would have to kill it in the bowl, my wife went and got something to crush it with.

"Leave it that way," I said. "Until morning."

"What if it gets out?"

"If it does, we'll let it go. We'll give it until morning. If it gets out, fine. If not, that means it's doomed and we kill it."

The washbasin was removed to a place where the constant rustling noise would not keep me awake.

The next morning, as soon as I woke up, I asked how the centipede was.

"Still there."

"Well, he's doomed then."

I had her bring the washbasin to me. The centipede seemed slightly weaker. This appeared in the sluggishness of its actions, particularly when it failed even to get as high as last night. No doubt about it—it was weaker.

"Let's wait until noon."

When I said this, I was thinking that the disaster which had befallen the centipede was completely fortuitous. It had fallen into this unluckiest of places, which it could not have known about. If I had struck and killed it in a place where it could fight back with all it had, both attack and defense would have been open and aboveboard. This was a misfortune that one could not even say was due to carelessness. I wanted, if I could, to save the centipede. Not by reaching out my hand and helping it—I wished to connive at its escaping from its dilemma by itself. So that I could say: "Come along now. You got out of it fair and square."

We waited until noon. It was the same thing. The centipede's fatigue was more noticeable. If it had been unable to get out with its full strength, there was certainly no hope it would now. Yet still I waited.

A desire to help and sympathy are different things. I felt not the least sympathy. It had nothing to do with the fact that the centipede was a pest. "As unfree as all that," I thought. I felt a restless irritation. Whereas the centipede was so daring and fierce in its familiar world of nature, a single misstep in man's world placed it at the mercy of the first trivial obstacle.

I had similar feelings toward people who had fallen into misfortune through no fault of their own. There were many among my friends who somehow or other compounded their bad luck, like a man who has stepped in a ditch at night. Of course, where people are involved there are complicated reasons. And yet it was a kind of annoyance that I felt toward them. I wanted to help. But there was no welling up of sympathy. That lack of sympathy was like my present state of mind.

By evening, the centipede had had enough. Even its stiff antennae waved feebly. There was the feeling of exhaustion, but it was nothing like the red frog which I had seen two years ago at Shuzenji. The red frog, trying to cross a rapid stream, had failed again and again. But rather than a difference of sky and mud between its exhaustion and the centipede's, it would be truer to say there was no comparison at all. Although defeated and broken, there was a beauty in the red frog. In the centipede, there was only a miserable ugliness. There had been a gallant spirit in the red frog.

Calling my wife, I told her to kill the centipede. Taking the basin into the garden, she dumped out the centipede and killed it. Did she want to see it crawl on the ground once more before it died? No sooner had the centipede touched its mother earth than it regained its energy, its proper dignity. My wife had been startled. When I heard about it, my heart failed me. I knew then that what I had done was unfair and cruel. But it was too late.

The Black Cat

When my illness was a little better, and I was able to read in bed, the first things that came to hand were travel books. Although I had always liked travel books, I had not read nearly as many as I might have. In talking with friends, too, I had found that travel books were surprisingly unread or at least not read anything like as much as other kinds of writing. There was no interest in reading a book about some place that had no apparent connection with one's own life and career; when one did try reading such books, few writers were able to make a totally unknown part of the world come alive; when, from a sort of nostalgia, one read about a previously visited place, the fact that one had been there enabled one to spot all the inaccuracies in the account. These were the usual reasons. I myself, while writing a kind of travel piece, had wondered who on earth would want to read it and thereby lost my self-confidence. Now, during my long spell in bed, I'd come to believe that the most avid readers of travel books must surely be invalids.

I read the old Japanese explorers Mamiya Rinzo, Matsuura Takeshiro, and Sugae Masumi. I read Goethe, Siebold, and the Swedish explorer Sven Hedin. Among the more modern, post-Meiji writers, I read at random whatever was in the house. When this scanty supply of books was exhausted, I read from a stack of geographic magazines placed by my pillow. Although I'd subscribed to this magazine for several years, until then the issues had simply piled up unread. However, now that I had an opportunity to peruse them at leisure and haphazardly open up and spread out their folds, I came to feel that there could be no greater pleasure than this.

In recent issues, there was a serialized account of a professor's travels in Sakhalin. It interested me. A passage about the Sakhalin lynx, a kind of wild cat that was all but extinct, worked strongly on my imagination. There had been captures of this great mountain cat in the forty-first year of Meiji, the first year of Taisho, and the fifth year of Showa. After that, it was thought to have become extinct. But then, in February of the sixteenth year of Showa, another was taken at a place called Noda. This last one was a female. When the hunter had sicked his dog on her, it was the dog that turned tail and fled. As the hunter raised his gun to shoot her, the lynx abruptly let fly with a stream of piss at him from a branch of the tree. Reading this matter-of-fact account over and over, I gazed insatiably at the photographs of lynxes that accompanied it. The lynxes in the photographs were the stuffed remains of those captured in the Meiji and Taisho periods. A caption said that in such things as the expression of the face they gave no idea of the live animal. Nonetheless, the truculence and ferocity said to be capable of knocking down a bear could be surmised from them. Measuring about one yard in length, the lynx had dark gray fur tinged with red and mottled with dark round spots. The fur was not long, but very dense-looking. The mouth seemed as if it would split the cheeks wide. On those cheeks, tufts of hairs grew out from the fur. The cat's whiskers were white and thick. But what bespoke its truculence the best were the limber, and if I can say it, the loglike four limbs of the beast. It must be a rule almost without exceptions that a leg is thicker at the top and thinner as it nears the ankle. It's said that with thickness of ankles quickness of movement is lost. But the legs of the lynx, from top to bottom, were just about the same thickness. Furthermore, in relation to the torso, they were astonishingly thick and also long. Not only did they not give the least feeling of sluggish slowness, they made you feel a flexible, savage strength. On such limbs, almost without a sound, the lynx paced about the island. In its toes were sheathed the razorlike hooked claws that could rip through a bear's gristle.

I imagined this dauntless animal, its eyes glittering, as it prowled the dense forests of Sakhalin. It was not known if throughout all the island even one or two survived. He was the last of his tribe, facing extinction. What loneliness must be his! And yet there was not a particle of the sad shadow that dogs loneliness. There was only a proud and haughty nature, full of fighting spirit. No matter what the circumstances, he never forfeited his birthright as king of the forest. When man, that lord of the earth, had aimed his gun at her, the lynx had not fled. Nor, honing the ultimate weapon of her hooked claws, had she bothered to stand her ground. From above the man's head, lifting her hind leg, she'd pissed on him and left it at that! For the lynx, that was all a man armed with a gun was worth.

Despite myself, I grinned broadly. To me, the bedridden invalid, the lynx had given the ultimate consolation. I received a gallant, braced feeling. One might almost call it a spiritual emotion.

In the same article, there was an account of the fur seals on Kaihyo Island. These, in diametrical contrast to the lynx, were a fine illustration of the biblical command to be fruitful and multiply. What one had here was bloody scuffles for the sake of reproduction. I'd once seen a movie about the gregarious seals. Bouncing around on their finlike flippers, emitting lugubrious noises like a bunch of sick cows—as I recalled them, I actually began to feel nauseated. Even the word for them, *ottosei*, suggestive of an Ottoman harem, was almost unbearably disgusting.

Just a few days after I'd been moved by the account of the lynx, a cat—it was only a stray cat, but in its arrogant demeanor there was a link between them—began to come and go around the house. It pleased me.

In the past two or three years, the number of cats and dogs hanging around our house had grown considerably. Of course, this was a result of the shortage of food among the human population. Some of these animals had been homeless all their lives, but many of them until quite recently had been pets. Their condition now was truly miserable and desperate. Those who'd had owners were so much worse off than the others. The dogs were worse off than the cats. In short, those who were the most used to living off people were the most wretchedly broken down. They came to forage in the garbage, but there was no such thing as garbage nowadays. Nonetheless, every day they would patiently come and hang around in the garden or by the kitchen door. The corner of the hedge, no matter how often we stopped it, always became a hole again without our knowing when. Maybe they thought that if they kept watch on the kitchen a hundred times they would come away one time with some food in their mouths. They also came to bask in the autumn sunshine, it seemed. It was my mother who disliked them the most. That was because the vegetable patch in the garden was her work, and they walked all over it.

By now, I was able to spend about fifteen minutes a day in the garden. I myself disliked having to go out there and look at them. I especially disliked the dogs. Curs that, when they had an owner, would have snarled at you if you so much as passed in front of their house now came up wagging their tails as if you were their long-lost friend. And yet never once did they take their eyes off your face. As soon as they'd sensed your unspoken antipathy, their tails dropped and drooped between their legs and with an unsteady, loping gait they fled. They wolfed rotten persimmons that had fallen off the tree. The cats, not so cringing as they, in the end became more shameless than a sneak thief. Not caring whether anyone was at home, they would invite themselves inside the house. Scampering through the rooms, they left their dirty paw-prints on the tatami. Perhaps recalling the good old days, they stretched themselves out at ease on the cushions. Yet when they saw that your eye was on them, they always ran away.

It was at this juncture that that cat appeared.

No one knew where it came from. It was a big black male, half

again the size of an ordinary cat. He had a truly lordly face. There
was authority in it. His tail was stubby. When you looked at him
from behind as he walked away, under the short tail and between the
haunches, very crisp and tight like a kind of hard fruit, not dangling
loosely but tautly bunched, his two big testes were like symbols of
the whole male sex. If he had any defect, it was the color of his fur. If
that had been lacquer black, what a magnificent cat he would have
been! Unfortunately, although I've said he was a black cat, he was a
drab, smudgy black tinged with dirty gray. When you saw that
dingy color, it made you think that his fate was after all as befitted the
lowly status of a stray cat.

He was absolutely unafraid of people. Even when your eye and
his met directly, he never ran away. He did not come inside the house
but, for instance, when I was lying on a long chair which I'd drawn
up to a window upstairs, he would come onto the roof right by my
head and, after staring into my face, stretch himself out at leisure in
the same sunny spot as myself. It was as if he had understood me. He
always walked with a slow, stately tread. Where did he get his food?
Yet he never acted as if he was hungry. He didn't seem to be on the
lookout for kitchen scraps.

"What a lordly tom," I said, impressed. "Hasn't he taken anything?"

"No, nothing yet," the people of the house answered.

"Give him something to eat now and then," I said. I even thought
that if times were better I might have made a pet of him.

It was the evening of the day when my folks had come up from the
country, bringing with them some salted salmon. For the first time
in so long, the fragrant smell of broiling salt-cured fish filled the
kitchen. Late that night I was awakened by a big ruckus downstairs.
Both my mother and wife were up. I could hear their voices in the
kitchen. After a while my wife came upstairs.

"What was it?"

"A cat. It got into the kitchen."

"But wasn't the door shut tight?"

"It got in from under the porch. It pushed up the trapdoor."

"Did it take anything?"

"No, it didn't, but that was only because Mother got up in time."

"Which cat was it?"

"We don't know. I have an idea it was that tiger-striped cat, but . . ."

So many cats hung around our place that there was no telling which one it had been. But none of us suspected the black cat.

The next night, there was the same kind of disturbance downstairs.

Accordingly, my wife and mother lifted a large round pickling stone onto the trapdoor and left it there. But that night also, the cat broke into the house in the same way, having heaved up even the heavy stone with his head. When my mother leapt out of bed and ran into the kitchen, he was already gone.

Making up names for the cat like "The Mysterious Midnight Thief," I was amused. But it was no joke for my mother and wife. More than anything, it was a serious disturbance of their much-needed rest.

The one who first began to suspect the black cat as the culprit was my mother. The animal that could break into the house by pushing up such a big pickling stone was the possessor of no mean strength. It was none other than the black cat. My mother was sure of it.

Certainly her belief had something to be said for it. But when I looked at the cat in question, I was incredulous. While these things were going on every night, every day, outside the house, the cat displayed absolutely the same demeanor as always. From the first jot to the last tittle, he was one cool old cat. He was too calm, too self-composed to be the nighttime intruder. With a certain meaning in my eye, I stared at him hard and long. But he looked back at me as if it had nothing to do with him.

Nevertheless, my mother would not change her mind.

Then one night, it was as if all hell had broken loose in the kitchen. Astonished, my wife jumped out of bed and ran downstairs. At this bigger than usual racket, I pricked up my ears despite myself. The uproar, starting out in the kitchen, worked its way into the bathroom next door. Amid the sounds of things banging and crashing to the floor, I heard the shrill voices of my mother and wife.

Presently, the noise died down.

"It's all right now. I'll take care of the rest. You go back to bed."

"You're sure it's all right?"

"It's all right, I tell you. Even this rascal can't do anything with this straw rope. I'll leave him this way for tonight . . . My, my, what a lot of fuss about nothing."

I heard my mother laugh.

My wife came back upstairs. Her face was slightly pale.

"Well, we caught him at last."

"You did? Which one was it?"

"It was the black cat after all."

"What? It was. . . ?"

"Mother drove him into the bathroom and beat him with a stick. When he flinched, she grabbed him and held him down. It was really something. He fought like a devil, a wildcat . . . So strong, he was."

"Yes, he would have been, if it was that cat. But it was he, was it? So it was he after all . . ."

The cat was tied up in the bathroom, my wife said. My mother had told her that she would take care of him herself. She did not want to make a young person touch him. Even so, my wife had been afraid. It was that time of year when the autumn nights are already rather cold. As if she were chilly, my wife crept back into bed.

I could not get back to sleep easily. The fact that it was he after all would not let me sleep. It was not that I felt this was so extraordinary, nor that I felt betrayed. What I did feel was a sort of intense smile that welled up to my lips. Perhaps it was one of admiration for his bold and willful behavior. Come to think of it, hadn't he, from start to finish, not raised a single cry? I realized that only now. I thought of him, tightly bound in the bathroom; there was never a cry nor any clatter. It even seemed as if he must have gotten away.

The next morning, my mother hauled him out of the bathroom and tied him up to a tree in back.

"What does Mother mean to do with him?"

"Kill him, of course. She says it's not something a young person should see. She won't let me come near."

I wondered if I should make a plea to my mother for the black cat's life. This fellow was worth it, I thought. I was drawn to his lonely pride that would not fawn on others. Doing that kind of thing by night, by day not giving himself away by so much as a hair out of place, not batting an eyelash when I looked at him—more than audacity, such intrepidity alone gave him a claim to be spared. If he were a human, I thought, by rights he would have been one of those country lords who brooked neither interference nor help. The fact that he was a stray cat was a prank of fate. His life was ruled by a happenstance, that of having dirty-colored fur. That was not anything he could have known about. It was a shame to humanity that while abjectly friendly creatures like dogs were given a warm place to sleep and things to eat, a cat like him had been thrown out. What was more, although he'd sunk so low in the world, he was not at all broken down and servile. *He* did not keep a furtive eye on the kitchen. Fair and square, he staged a daring night attack, fought as hard as he could, and the moment he was taken did not struggle in his bonds or even cry out.

But I could not say any of this to my mother. In our life as it was, such thoughts were no more than an invalid's luxury. This spring also, I'd had a little difference with my mother. In the garden of this rented house of ours, there were several trees, such as an oak, a maple, a cherry tree, and a banana tree. From springtime into the season of full green leafage, the trees all had beautiful shapes. I liked to move my sickbed to a place from which I could see them. But then, once, my mother had lopped and cut back the branches of those trees without mercy. It was painful even to watch her. Some of the trees ended up looking like close-cropped heads of priests. I was angry. But then I immediately apologized in my heart. It was not that my mother had no love for the trees. It was not that she didn't understand the beauty of the trees and shrubs. But my mother had to let the sun shine in on the vegetable patch that she had made. Working the hoe from her bent waist, shouldering buckets of night soil, she tilled every corner of the small garden and made it like a fruitful field. Her sole desire was to provide fresh vegetables for her ailing son.

It was not that I did not recognize, reluctantly, that in the search for food the relationship between people and cats had become a struggle in which no love was lost. It had become difficult, when something was taken, to smile and shrug it off as in the past. Even the thirty minutes of sleep lost every night was not, for my mother and wife, the small thing that it once would have been. There was no margin left for me, the invalid, to rescue the black cat, saying I liked him because he was an outcast . . . Also, when I tried to think that if he was punished once like this he would have learned his lesson, I had to admit I was being softheaded. Because he was not, of course, that kind of docile creature.

In the afternoon, taking my prescribed nap, I dozed a little without actually falling asleep. My wife, who'd gone to get our rations, was a long time coming back. As soon as I woke up, I thought about the black cat again. My mother, as was her habit on fine days, would have gone out today also to spend the day digging in the garden. I listened closely, but as before there were no sounds like that out back. When my wife came upstairs she said at once:

"Mother has already taken care of it. When I got back just now, I glanced under the banana tree. It was wrapped up in a straw mat. Its paws were sticking out a little . . ."

My wife made a face, as if she had seen something which she ought not to have seen.

I wondered what method my mother had used. At times the feelings of old people are extremely sentimental, but at other times they're unemotional almost to the point of callousness. Most likely my mother had disposed of the cat with the nonchalance peculiar to the old. And yet, even at his last moment, hadn't the cat raised an anguished "gyaaa"? At any rate, it was lucky that I had been napping and my wife out on an errand. Perhaps my mother had chosen that time on purpose.

86

In the evening, my mother was out of the house for a short while. During that time, the straw-wrapped bundle disappeared from under the banana tree.

From the next day, I once again went out into the sunny garden for fifteen or twenty minutes a day. The black cat gone, only craven mutts and strays dragged themselves around. Foolish and inferior, they were as tiresome as my illness, which there was no knowing when it would go away. I began to despise them more than I had up to then.

The Wasps

Some lively visitors to my sickroom in early summer were the wasps. Certainly the stately, dashing appearance of the wasps befitted the forerunners of an active, prosperous season. Even the melancholy sickroom seemed suddenly to acquire an air of gaiety. The wasps were never still. Of course not when they were flying around but even when they alighted, a brimful energy kept their bodies pulsing as they moved about in short, mincing steps. A waist narrow as a thread connected their chests and abdomens. At first sight their bodies seemed all an elegant slenderness, but in fact they possessed a flexible toughness and durability. Judging from their exiguous midriffs, you might think they could be easily pulled apart or snapped in two like a twig, but I doubt if they could. They had a steely luster about them, which partook not of iron blackness but of a beautiful, gleaming blue. Their wings, too, as they took the light, were a lovely glistening purple. There was a persimmon tree that reached down its branches an arm's length away from my sickroom window. Its small white flowers were falling now. The honeybees hummed about it busily, as if time were short. Compared with the wasps, they seemed like hardworking, honest citizens. Those mountain bandits, the hornets, were more like good-natured peasants. The wasps were like mettlesome samurai, out for glory. Once a wasp that I had just seen zoom up to the ceiling, with a resonant buzz that I couldn't believe was his, dive-bombed my pillow. No time to think that it was the wasp of just now—it was like a black pebble flung hard at me. It seemed to fly straight at my face. I threw up my right hand. I knew it was the wasp when it levelled off with a droning noise. It landed with a corpulent horsefly that lay on its side with its legs loosely bunched. As I watched, the fly gave a few spastic twitches. After a while it could not move at all. Embracing the big horsefly with its whole body—head, legs, and stinger—the wasp gave it the coup de grace. They rolled over together like a burr.

Another time I saw a wasp caught in a spider's web under the eaves. It was a freshly made web, as yet unbroken. "Now you're caught," I thought. Just then the wasp, with a violent shuddering and buzzing, adroitly made its escape from the web. As if nothing had happened, it flew up toward the high summer sky. The spider, who had instantly glided down from its hiding place in the upper part of the web, seemed as surprised as myself to find its likely prey gone. That sort of resolute quickness was just like the wasps.

But there were so many of them! Busily spelling each other in their labors—not even the flies, whose numbers abruptly increased at this time, could compare with them. "So many wasps!" my human visitors would say, their eyes widening as they suddenly noticed them all. Was there a reason why the wasps liked my room?

In the lintel and window-posts of the paper door, there were a lot of little round holes. Up to now, I had not cared at all what they were, or when and why they'd been made. This was an old, remodelled farmhouse and they were just naturally there. Why they were naturally there had never occurred to me. It was only as I lay in bed day after day that I saw there was a special relationship between those holes and the wasps. When they flew in the room and alighted on the lintel or the sides of the window, the wasps walked around as if looking for something. When they found one of those holes, they always went inside it. Not once but four or five times, they came out and went back in. They seemed to conduct a minute inspection tour around each and every hole. Then they went inside. Then they came out again. The wasps were clearing some kind of trash out of the holes. In it was mixed what looked like fragments of insect wings. The holes were evidently deep enough to conceal four-fifths of the wasps' bodies. The wasps took fairly long with their housecleaning. Afterward they would fly out of the room. When one wasp came back, I saw that it was carrying something between its legs, perhaps a small, winged insect. Its legs still locked around its prey, the wasp entered the hole. When it had stored its booty in there, it flew away. But it was back again soon, with a new victim. This time it was something as big as the wasp itself. When I looked closely, it seemed to be a small grasshopper. Unhurriedly, the wasp pushed it inside the hole. The third time, it brought back a green caterpillar or grub. If it could hold so much, the hole must be larger than I'd thought. Most likely it wound its way back to a hollowed chamber. The wasp flew away again. By now, however, the summer's day was at an end. The wasp did not come back again.

The next day, the wasp was back by the time I'd finished breakfast. I had wondered if it would repeat the previous day's routine. As I watched, it circled and recircled the hole as if on the lookout for something. Slowly drawing the circle tighter, it circumspectly approached the hole. This time it entered not head first but by backing itself in. Once its hindquarters were inside, it stopped so that its front half protruded from the hole.

For a while it continued quietly in that pose. Quietly but not idly, as I saw when I looked closer. It was in the midst of some work that was very important to it. Now and then it would move just slightly. Then it would be still again. While straining its whole body to accomplish one thing, the wasp constantly looked about it as if for enemies that might do it harm. There was a stillness about the wasp that I could not have imagined as other than of death. I thought that its strange little face expressed an unusual seriousness. Clearly this work had to do with life . . . at last even I understood. The wasp was laying its eggs.

It was a long hard job. Finally the wasp came all the way out of the hole. Eased of its burden, it showed its relief at having discharged an important duty by wagging its abdomen up and down. Again it patrolled the area around the hole. Then it flew away. When it came back again, it had something else. Thrusting its head in along with whatever it was, the wasp labored intently in the hole. When it backed out again, I was surprised. The mouth of the hole had been beautifully sealed with something like mud. A white, beautiful mud wall. I realized that what the wasp had brought before was a crumb of dirt, that it had mixed this with its own secretion and plastered up the hole. And yet, how had it achieved such whiteness? Had it kneaded its own honey into the earth?

Just as if well pleased with itself, the wasp waved its feelers around. Then, with a sonorous buzzing, it flew away.

The next day, it came by again. When it had made sure that everything was all right, it buzzed away again.

I now looked at the other holes. I saw that all of them had been plastered over in the same way.

We were midway through a torrid August. The heat that summer was the worst in many years. Already ill, I was laid low by the heat. It had worn me out to watch the wasp go about its little business for two days. The same vitality that had cheered me up in early summer now got on my nerves. Even what had been self-evident from the start, that these lively activities were on behalf of reproduction, was now repulsive to me. What if I poked a twig or straw through those white walls? I had such thoughts. No doubt if I'd been well enough to get up I would have acted on my bad impulse. It oppressed me to think that next year those eggs would hatch out. If I thought ahead even so far as a month, the future seemed vague and hazardous. But then, I also steeped myself in grandiose dreams of my life ten or twenty years from now. It seemed to me that this sort of inconsistency was a sign that my illness was getting worse. I thought of the theory that hopelessly ill persons are apt to indulge themselves in grand dreams of the future. And yet I found a pleasure, an ease of heart, in developing such dreams and dwelling on their details.

The summer passed, and autumn became winter. My lively insect-companions also went away. A few, however, were left. Flies in winter were not unusual. But what was I to make of soldier bugs in winter, and praying mantises? Until early December, you could see praying mantises by the roadside, dragging themselves along as if on stilts. But I would find them clinging to my paper door until the end of January. As for the soldier bugs, they lasted into February. They had lost all their summer greenness—perhaps it was a different species—and were now the color of shrivelled turnip leaves. There was no trace of that smelly froth that soldier bugs exude. In the afternoon, I would place a rattan chaise longue by the south-facing window and lie on it in the sun. Then I would notice that the soldier bugs had moved along with me. Maybe a foot away from my face, they lined up companionably. We stayed there until the sun went down.

One day, I slid open the window in front of my writing table. Something like small beans fell pit-a-pat onto the table. They were ladybugs. A bevy of them had chosen to spend the winter in the warmth of my room. Soon they were everywhere: on the paper door, on the desk, and even on my books. Bearing on their black shards the rising sun of Japan, they continued their lively promenade. Some even crawled up on my bedding.

With such friendly insects, I spent the winter indoors. During that time my illness hung in the balance.

The warm time of the year came around again. One day, I heard a familiar spirited buzzing noise. It startled me. My heart beat faster. I'd forgotten all about the wasps. At the sudden memory, I looked across the room at last year's holes. Slowly sitting up, I dragged myself toward them. I examined the white, sealed entrance of one of the holes. A tiny aperture had been punched through its mud-paper wall. I looked at the other holes. Each had been broken out of, and was empty again.

Meanwhile the sound of buzzing, of one, two, and more winged insects, grew steadily louder and stronger. Soon it was everywhere in the room. For the first time, my weakened body and mind were filled by the joy of being alive.

HAYASHI FUMIKO

[1904–1951]

A Late Chrysanthemum

After the phone call saying that he would come at five that evening, Kin, thinking it's been a year, can it be that long, coming away from the phone and looking at her watch, saw there were still about two hours until five. Before anything else, she must take a bath. Having the maid make preparations for an early supper, Kin hurried to the bathhouse. She must look even more youthful than she had that time when they parted. It would be a defeat if she let him feel her age. Having taken her time in the bath, as soon as she came back Kin wrapped some crushed ice in a double piece of gauze. For about ten minutes at the mirror, she massaged her face evenly with the ice. Her skin grew red and numb, so that she could not feel a thing. The age of a woman who was fifty-six years old bared its fangs in her heart. But Kin, with the discipline of long years of practice in concealing such things as her age, rubbed her cold face with the precious imported cream. In the mirror, the bluish aged face of a dead woman opened its eyes wide. Midway in her makeup, Kin felt a sudden dislike of her own face. Her charming, beautiful figure of the past, which had been featured on postcards, rose up behind her eyes. Pulling up her skirts, she looked at the flesh of her thighs. They had not the full, swelling ripeness they had once had. Fine capillaries stood out on their surface. But it was a consolation that they had not lost that much of their firm fleshiness. Her thighs fitted together snugly. In the bath, Kin always poured water into the hollow of her primly seated thighs. The hot water collected and stayed in their little ditch. Relief and ease of heart solaced Kin for her age. She could still get a man. That alone, she felt, was a source of strength for living. Parting her thighs, Kin quietly stroked their inner sides as if they were someone else's. Their softness was that of chamois, sleek and suppled with oil. In an old story by Saikaku it was told that among the sights of Ise were two samisen-playing beauties called Osugi and Tama. Before they played, a crimson netting was put up and coins tossed in at their faces through the holes of the net. Remembering the story, the crimson netting, Kin had the unbearable feeling that for her that kind of beauty, like a colored woodblock print, had already become a thing of the faraway past. In her youth, Kin had been steeped in the flesh, her eyes darkened by the love of money. But with the years, and especially in ducking the waves of the terrible war, Kin had come to feel that life without a man was empty and comfortless. With age her beauty had changed, little by little, and its character had come to be different. Kin as she got older did not commit the folly of wearing flashy clothes. The strange artfulness of women over fifty who wore necklaces over their meager bosoms, skirts whose red checked pattern was more suitable for a waistcloth, large, droopy white satin blouses, and wide-brimmed hats to hide the wrinkles on their brows was distasteful to Kin. She also disliked the affectation of the geisha-prostitute who lets the red of her neck cloth be glimpsed.

Until this period, Kin had never worn foreign clothes. A pure, bracing white crepe collar, a lined kimono of Oshima indigo splash pattern, an obi of thin cream-colored white-striped Hakata. Never to show the water-colored sash bustle under the breasts. Building up the solid fullness of the bosom, the hips slender. Fastening her underthings tightly with an undersash, she placed a "back cushion" of thinly covered silk floss against her buttocks. It reminded her of the stylish dressing-up of Western women. Her hair had always had a brownish tinge, and with her fair complexion did not seem that of a woman past fifty. Perhaps because the large-bodied Kin wore her kimono tight-skirted, it gave a clean, spruce effect. Always before meeting a man she made herself ready in this sober, professional manner. At the mirror she drank down several cups of cold sake. Then she brushed her teeth, making sure to kill her sake-laden breath. Just a little bit of sake had more effect on her than any amount of cosmetics. As a faint inebriation rose up in her, her eyes became slightly bloodshot and watery. The gloss of her face, which she had made up lightly over a base of cream dissolved with glycerin, was as fresh and young-looking as if life had been breathed back into it. Only the lipstick, a refined dark shade, she painted on thickly. Her lips were the only crimson part of her. Kin had never in her life worn even nail polish. Now that her hands were old, such adornment would have been all the more wishful, jejune, and ludicrous. Simply rubbing latex over the back of her hands, clipping the nails so short it almost hurt, she buffed them with wool scraps. As for the colors that were to show at the openings of her sleeves, wanting them all to be pale hues, Kin put on a shaded pattern of pink and blue stripes. For perfume, she rubbed a sweetish scent over her shoulders and her fleshy arms. Never, even by mistake, did she dab any on her earlobes. Kin did not want to forget that she was a woman. Rather than the dirtiness of an old lady of the world, it would be better to be dead. —"So unhappy, I'd do what a woman shouldn't; think of a rose, that's me." Kin was fond of this popular song. Even thinking about a life apart from men made her shudder. As she looked at the pale pink petals of the roses that Itaya had brought, in their extravagance Kin dreamt of the past. It was even a pleasure to her that the customs of the distant past, her tastes and amusements, had slowly changed. On nights when she slept alone and woke up in the small hours, Kin would secretly count on her fingers the number of men since her girlhood. That man, that man, and then that man, ah, and that man too . . . but that man, maybe I met him before that man . . . or maybe it was afterward . . . in this counting song of memory, Kin's heart grew smoky and stifled. There were women whose tears came according to how they'd parted from a man. Kin liked to think only of when she'd met each man. Perhaps because she stored up in her heart the memories of men of the old days, in the manner of the *Tales of Ise* which she'd once read, Kin, in her solitary bed, enjoyed drowsily musing on the men of her past. —The phone call from Tabé had been unexpected. It had been like setting eyes on a glass of fine wine. Tabé himself was coming because he was lured on by a memory. Sentimentally thinking that there must be something left of the past, he was coming to scrutinize the burnt-out traces of love. It would not do, standing in a field of rubble, to merely make him sigh. There must not be the slightest sign of paucity either in her age or in her surroundings. A discreet expression was more important than anything. The atmosphere must be that of a floating world in which the two could immerse themselves. Tabé must not be allowed to forget the aftertaste of memory, that his woman was always a beautiful woman. When she'd finished dressing herself without a hitch, Kin stood at the mirror and made sure of her dancing-figure. Was everything as it should be? . . . Going into the tea-room, Kin found the supper trays already set out. Sitting across from the maid, she had some watery miso shiru, salted kelp, and barley rice. Afterward, breaking an egg, she drank down the yolk. In the past, even when a man came visiting, Kin had not often served supper herself. It was the farthest thing from her mind to set up the dining table and enumerate all the things she had cooked so as to be thought lovable. Kin had no interest in being a domestic woman. There was no reason to play herself up as such to a man who was not even thinking of marriage. The men who came before Kin came bearing gifts. For Kin, this was as it should be. Kin never made friends with a man who had no money. There was nothing so charmless as a man without money. A man courting her favor who, under a Western suit that hadn't even been brushed, calmly wore long johns with the buttons missing, suddenly became repulsive. Kin's feeling about the man's attentions themselves was that, one by one, they built up a collection of beautiful objects. In her girlhood, Kin had been said to resemble Manryu, a famous geisha of Akasaka.

Once, she had seen Manryu after the latter's marriage. She was an enchantingly beautiful woman. Kin had moaned with admiration of that splendid beauty. She'd realized then that for a woman to always retain her beauty, there must be money. Kin had become a geisha in her nineteenth year. She hadn't had many accomplishments, but had been able to become a geisha through her beauty alone. One time, she had been called to the house of a rather aged Frenchman who had come to see the Orient. Made much of by the old gentleman as the Marguerite Gautier of Japan, Kin herself had affected that role of the Dame aux Camélias. In his physical attentions, the man had been unexpectedly bothersome. Somehow, though, he was a man whom it was hard to forget. His name was Michel, and no doubt by now he had died somewhere in the north of France. After his return home, he'd sent Kin a bracelet inlaid with opals and small diamonds. It was the one thing she had not let go of, even at the height of the war. — The men with whom Kin had had relations had all gone on to become well-known. But in this postwar period, she had not even heard any news of most of them. Although it was rumored that Aizawa Kin had amassed a considerable fortune, Kin had never thought of opening a teahouse or a restaurant. Her property had consisted of a house that had come through the firebombings unscathed and a cottage in Atami. She was not as rich as people said. Taking advantage of its being registered in her younger sister-in-law's name, she had seen her opportunity and sold the cottage after the war. Though completely useless, her maid Kinu had been given her by her sister-in-law. She was a deaf-mute. Kin led a surprisingly modest life. She never felt like going to see a movie or a play, and she disliked going outside without a purpose. It was unpleasant to have her age exposed to the sun and seen by others. In the bright sunlight, the pathos of an old woman was mercilessly displayed. Even the most expensive clothes and jewelry, under the sun, were no good whatsoever. Kin was content to live as a flower in the shade. One of her pleasures was reading novels. Although it had been suggested to her that she adopt a daughter and consider the comforts of old age, Kin did not like to think of such things as old age. And Kin had a reason for having lived alone until now. —Kin had no parents. All she remembered was that she had been born in Osunagawa, near Hanjo in Akita. At five years of age she had been taken to Tokyo to live with the Aizawa family. Given their surname, she had grown up as a daughter of the house. Aizawa Kyujiro had been her foster father, but when Kin was a schoolgirl he'd gone to Dairen on a public works project and had never been heard of again. Her foster mother, Ritsu, had been quite a businesswoman, speculating on the stock market and building houses for rent. At that time they lived in the Street of the Straw Shops in Ushigomé. The Aizawas of the Straw Street had been regarded even in Ushigomé as rather wealthy people. In Kagurazaka there had been an old Japanese sock-maker's called the Tatsui. They had a beautiful daughter called Machiko. It was a shop with a tradition equal to that of the Myogawa in Ningyocho. Even in the residential district of the Yamanote, people trusted the reputation of the Tatsui for socks. In the spacious shop-front, under the dark blue curtains, Machiko, wearing a black satin collar with her hair done up in the "peach-cleft" style, worked the treadle of a sewing machine. Even among the students of Waseda University she was famous, it seemed. Some of them were said to tip Machiko when they came to give an order. Kin, who was five or six years younger than this Machiko, was also famous in the neighborhood as a beautiful girl. The two of them were known as the belles of Kagurazaka. — When Kin was nineteen, a speculator named Torigoe had the run of the Aizawa house. The family began to go downhill. Ritsu developed a habit of drinking herself into a frenzy. A dark life continued for a long time. Because of a chance joke, Kin was violated by Torigoe. In desperation, she fled the house and came out as a geisha from an establishment in Akasaka. As for Machiko of the Tatsui, riding in one of the newfangled airplanes in a long-sleeved kimono and crashing on the Susaki Plain, she became known all over the country when the incident appeared in the newspapers. Kin had taken a professional name. Her photograph soon appeared in fiction magazines and eventually on one of the postcards popular at the time.

Thought of now, these things had all become the things of the remote past. Yet Kin could not comprehend that she was actually a woman over fifty. Though there were times when she thought, "I've lived a long time," there were also times when she felt her life had been like a brief spring. After Ritsu died, the remains of the family fortune were inherited by Kin's younger foster sister Sumiko, who'd been born after Kin's adoption. This had cleared Kin of any further obligation to the family.

Kin had met Tabé at the time Sumiko and her husband were running a boardinghouse for students. Leaving her employer of three years, she'd taken a room at Sumiko's place. The life there was pleasant. By now the Pacific War had started. Getting to know the student Tabé whom she'd met in Sumiko's parlor, at some point she'd begun a relationship with this Tabé (who was young enough to be her son) that they concealed from others. To those who did not know her, the fifty-year-old Kin looked only thirty-seven or so. There was a youthful fragrance about her thick eyebrows. Tabé, soon after his graduation, went to the front as a second lieutenant in the army. For a while his unit was stationed in Hiroshima. Kin visited him twice there.

As soon as she'd arrived, Tabé had come to the inn in his military uniform. Although flinching at the leathery smell of his body, Kin had spent two nights with him. Exhausted by her journey to this distant place, she'd been battered by Tabé's masculine strength. She had confessed to friends that she had felt like dying. After these two visits, even though Tabé had sent telegrams several times, Kin did not go to Hiroshima again. In the seventeenth year of Showa, Tabé was posted to Burma. In May of the year after the end of the war, he was repatriated. Immediately coming up to Tokyo, he'd called on Kin in her house in Numabukuro. But he had aged terribly. As Kin looked at the gaps where his front teeth had been, even the dream of the past disappeared in her disappointment. Tabé, a native of Hiroshima, had an elder brother in the Diet. Having started an automobile dealership in Tokyo with his brother's help, within a year he had become an unrecognizably splendid entrepreneur. Appearing before Kin, he spoke of taking a wife in the near future. After that, for more than a year now, Kin had not seen him. —When the air raids had been at their heaviest, Kin, buying this house in Numabukuro with installed telephone at a throwaway price, had evacuated from Totsuka. Although it wasn't at all far from Totsuka, Kin's house in Numabukuro had survived while Sumiko's house in Totsuka had burnt down. Sumiko and her family had fled to Kin's place for refuge. But at the end of the war, Kin had driven them out. Of course, Sumiko had immediately built a house on the burnt-out site in Totsuka, and now if anything felt grateful to Kin. Looking back, one could see that it had been possible to build cheaply right after the war.

When she'd sold the cottage in Atami, with the profit of nearly three hundred thousand yen Kin would buy run-down houses, fix them up, and sell them for three or four times what she'd paid. Kin was not flustered by money. She'd learned from long years of observation that as long as you kept cool, money increased itself like a ball of snow rolling downhill. She even lent money at low rates, securing it with good collateral. Having lost faith in banks since the war, Kin kept her money in circulation as much as possible. She was not so foolish as to hide it under a mattress like a farmer. She employed Sumiko's husband as her agent. Kin knew also that if you gave them a percentage, people cheerfully went about your business. Living alone with her maid in a house of four rooms might seem lonely to an outsider's eye, but Kin was not the least bit lonely. Since she did not like to go out, she did not even think the life of two women alone inconvenient. Rather than keeping a dog against burglars, she believed in firmly shut doors. The doors of Kin's house were more securely fastened than those of any other house in the neighborhood. The maid being deaf and dumb, no matter what man came, there was no fear of being overheard. And yet there were times when Kin wondered about her fate, which might be to be tragically murdered. Holding her breath, she would think uneasily of the dead-quiet house. Kin never forgot to keep the radio on from morning to night. At about this time, Kin had made the acquaintance of a man who had a flower garden in Matsudo of Chiba. A younger brother of the person who'd bought the Atami cottage, he had set up a trading company in Hanoi during the war. Repatriated afterward, with his brother's capital he had started his flower farm in Matsudo. He was still only about forty, but was completely bald and looked older than his years. His name was Itaya Kiyotsugu. He had come to see Kin two or three times about the cottage, and at some point had begun to visit her once a week. After Itaya started calling, Kin's house was gay with gifts of beautiful flowers. —Today, also, a yellow Castanian rose had been put in a vase in the alcove. "Falling gingko leaves and sweet memories, damp frost in the rose garden." The yellow rose made Kin think of the beauty of a mature woman. It was in some song. The fragrance of the rose on the damp, cold mornings brought poignant memories into Kin's heart. When the phone call came, Kin realized that she was more drawn to the young Tabé than to Itaya. At Hiroshima it had been painful, but Tabé had been a soldier then. His rough youthfulness, now, seemed nothing excessive. It was a touching, happy memory. Even harsh memories, with time, somehow became dear. —It was well past five when Tabé came, carrying a big bundle. Taking things such as whiskey, ham, and cheese from the bundle, he sat down with a thud in front of the long brazier. Already, there was not a trace of his former youthfulness. In his gray checked jacket and blackish green pants, he looked like a garage attendant. "You're as beautiful as ever." "Oh, thank you. But it's all over for me." "No, you're more sexy than my wife." "Is your wife young?" "Yes, but she's a farm girl." Taking a cigarette from Tabé's silver case, Kin let him light it for her. The maid came in with whiskey glasses and the ham and cheese heaped up together on a plate. "A good-looking girl . . ." Tabé spoke with a broad grin. "Yes, but she's a deaf-mute." With an "aha" expression, Tabé stared at the girl's figure. Gentle-eyed, the girl politely bowed her head to him. For Kin, the unnoticed youthfulness of the maid suddenly became an eyesore. "How have you been?" Tabé blew out the cigarette smoke. Then, with a look of "ah—my own news," he said, "We're expecting a child next month." "Oh, is that so?" Kin, holding the bottle of whiskey, poured some into Tabé's glass. Tabé, emptying his glass with an air of relishing its contents, poured some into Kin's glass. "You have a good life." "Oh? How?" "Although the storm blows and rages outside, you alone, no matter how much time goes by, are the same . . . You're a strange person. Of course, in your case, you probably have a good patron, but women have it easy." "Are you being sarcastic? But I've never caused you any inconvenience, have I, to have that kind of thing said to me?" "Are you mad at me? I didn't mean it that way. I'm saying you're a lucky person. A man's life is hard, and so I just said that kind of thing. In today's world, one cannot live carelessly. Either eat or be eaten. People like me live by gambling every day." "But your business is doing well, isn't it?" "No, it's not . . . Money is tight. It's like a tightrope act, with ringing in your ears." Kin silently licked up her whiskey. A cricket singing at the base of the wall sounded unpleasantly damp. Tabé, when he'd drunk his second glass of whiskey, roughly seized Kin's hand across the brazier. Her hand, wearing no ring, was as soft and limp as a silk handkerchief. Withdrawing the strength from her fingertips, Kin held her breath. Its strength withheld, the hand's softness had a cold fleshiness. In Tabé's drunken eyes, the things of the past whirled in a maelstrom and engulfed his heart. In all her past beauty the woman sat before him. It was a strange feeling. In the ceaseless flowing of the months and years, little by little experience accumulated. One either leapt into the current or fell into it. But a woman of his past, unchanged in any way, solidly sat there. Tabé stared at Kin's face. Even the wrinkles around her eyes were the same. Her profile hadn't sagged. He wanted to know the circumstances of this woman's life. Perhaps, in this woman, there had been no response to the reverberations of the times. Displaying her clothes chest, her long brazier, the luxurious profusion of her roses, smiling serenely, she sat before him. Though she must already be over fifty, there was a fragrant womanliness about her. Tabé did not know Kin's actual age. The disheveled, exhausted figure of his wife, just turned twenty-five, rose up behind the apartment-dweller Tabé's eyes. Kin, from a drawer of the brazier, took out a delicate Japanese pipe of beaten silver and, fitting the stub of a plain cigarette in the bowl, lighted it. Tabé was knocking his kneecaps together every now and then. It annoyed her. Thinking that he might be in financial straits, she observed his face intently. The simpleminded love of the times when she'd gone to Hiroshima had already faded out of Kin's heart. The long blank between them, now that they had met, gave her an unsettled feeling. She felt irritated and lonely. Her heart just did not flare up for him as in the past. She even had the thought that perhaps by knowing this man's body the man had lost all glamour for her. It irked her that although the atmosphere was there, the feeling of love itself did not flare up. "Isn't there a friend of yours who could lend me four hundred thousand or so?" "Oh? Is it money? Four hundred thousand is a lot, isn't it?" "Uh, yes, that's how much I need. Can't you think of something?" "No, I can't. Isn't it unreasonable to come to me with that kind of thing? I don't make any money." "Is that so? I'll pay you good interest. How about it?" "No! It's unfair to talk to me that way." Kin suddenly felt a chill of fear. Her peaceful relationship with Itaya began to seem precious. Feeling downcast, she took the pebbled iron teapot which was bubbling briskly and poured herself tea. "Can't you somehow lend me two hundred thousand? I'll be forever grateful . . ." "You're a strange man, aren't you? Talking to me about money although you must know perfectly well I don't have any. I need some myself. You didn't come because you wanted to see me, did you? You came to ask me for money." "No, I wanted to see you, I wanted to see you. But I thought that if it was you I could talk about anything, so . . ." "You should talk to your elder brother." "I can't talk to my brother about this money." Kin didn't answer. Abruptly, she thought, I'll only be young another two or three years. Their love, which in the past had burned like the summer sun, had no warmth for them now, she realized. Perhaps it hadn't been love but the bond of male and female that had strongly pulled them together. The brittle bond between men and women, like a fallen leaf drifting in the wind. For herself, sitting here, and Tabé, it had become the meaningless bond of acquaintance. A cold feeling began to flow in Kin's heart. As she drank her tea, Tabé, as if he'd remembered something, grinning, said in a low voice, "Is it all right if I stay?" Her eyes surprised, Kin smiled, purposely bringing out the wrinkles at their corners. "It's no good. Please don't tease me." Her beautiful white false tooth gleamed. "You're cruel. I'm not talking about money now. I'm paying court to the Kin-san of yore. —It's a different world in here. You've been through your hard times. Not to have gone under, no matter what happened—that's remarkable . . . The young women nowadays are pathetic. Hey, do you dance?" Kin laughed at the back of her nose. Young women, indeed. It was not anything she knew about. "I don't know how to dance. And you?" "Some." "You must have a good partner. Doesn't that take money?" "Don't be a fool. I don't make that kind of easy money that I can keep a woman." "But you're dressed like a gentleman. Unless you had a good job, you couldn't do that." "This is just a front. Actually, I'm broke. I have to scrounge just to get enough to eat . . ." Kin smothered a laugh. She was fascinated by Tabé's bushy black hair. Locks of it hung down over his forehead. The fragrant freshness of his student days was gone, but around his cheeks there was an aura of middle-aged manly glamour. Even though it wasn't a refined face, there was something strong in it. Alertly observant, like an animal who has detected a scent from afar, Kin poured out some tea for Tabé. "Is it true they're going to devalue the money soon?" She spoke as if joking. "Do you have enough to worry about?" "My! You changed your tack suddenly. Right back on money. I just asked because there are rumors going around." "Well, with Japan in the shape it's in, I don't see how they can. Anyway, people with no money don't have to worry." "Really . . . ?" Kin merrily poured more whiskey into Tabé's glass. "Ahh—I'd like to go to some quiet place like Hakoné. I'd like to sleep for three days in a place like that." "Are you tired?" "It's this worry about money." "But isn't it like you to worry about money? As long as it's not about some woman . . ." Tabé was rankled by Kin's prim manner. It was even funny, as if he were looking at a high-class antique. If I slept with her tonight, he thought, it would be like giving alms to the poor. He stared at her chin. Its firm line showed her strength of will. The fresh youthfulness of the deaf-mute maid whom he'd seen earlier rose up behind his eyelids, curiously doubled. She was no beauty, but her youth, to an eye trained on women like Tabé's, was vivid and vital. If this lukewarm encounter with Kin were their first, there would be none of this stickiness about it. Tabé felt the age in Kin's face, where even more than before the weariness showed. Kin—had she guessed something?—abruptly got to her feet and went into the next room. Going to the mirror stand, she took the hypodermic syringe for hormone injections and jabbed herself in the arm. Rubbing the skin hard with a piece of absorbent cotton, she peered into the mirror and patted the bridge of her nose with a powder puff. Men and women between whom there was no quickening love had tiresome encounters like this. Unexpected tears, like the ghosts of her mortified regret, rose up behind Kin's eyelids. If it had been Itaya, she could have plunged her weeping face into his lap. She could have been the child with him. Kin didn't know whether she liked or disliked this Tabé who sat at the brazier. She wanted him to go away, and yet there was the restless desire to leave a little more of herself in his heart. Tabé's eyes, since he'd parted from her, had seen many women. After going to the privy, on her way back she glanced in at the maid's room. Kinu, cutting out patterns from newspaper pages, was hard at work on her Western sewing lesson. Her big buttocks planted firmly on the tatami, she leaned over the newspaper plying her scissors. Her nape, beneath the exactly coiled hair, was white and lustrous. Her firm, full body was alluring. Kin returned to her seat at the brazier. Tabé lay sprawled out. Kin turned on the radio on top of the tea chest. Unexpectedly loud, Beethoven's Ninth Symphony poured out into the room. Tabé jerked himself upright. He put the whiskey glass to his lips again. "You and I went to Shibamata once. It rained into the inn, and we ate eels without rice." "Yes, that's how it was then. Food was already scarce. It was before you became a soldier. Red lilies were blooming in the alcove. Do you remember how we knocked the vase over?" "That kind of thing . . ." Kin's face had suddenly filled out and become youthful. "Shall we go again some time?" "Yes, let's . . . but it's already too much bother. Even there you could have anything you liked, now, couldn't you?" Kin, as though not to lose the tearful sentimentality of before, silently tried to reel in the memories of the past. But it was the face of a man other than Tabé that surfaced in her heart. After she'd gone to Shibamata with Tabé, just after the war, she remembered, she had gone there once with a man named Yamazaki. Yamazaki had died recently during a stomach operation. The dusky room on the bank of the Edogawa, the sultry late-summer day, came back to her. She could hear the steady, clunking sound of the automatic irrigation pump, the cicada's ascending cry. Outside the window, their silver hubcaps glittering, the cars of food hunters raced along the high embankment. Although it was her second rendezvous with Yamazaki, his virginal youthfulness had seemed like something holy to Kin. There'd been plenty to eat, and it had been quiet, as if the dispirited postwar world had suddenly been hung in a void. She remembered the evening trip back on the bus along the broad military highway. "After that, did you meet any interesting people?" "Me?" "Yes." "Except for you, there were no interesting people." "Liar!" "Oh? How? Isn't it true? Who would take up with somebody like me?" "I don't believe you." "Oh, well, from now on I intend to blossom out and make my life worth living." "Because you still have quite a ways to go, eh?" "Yes, I mean to live a long time, until I fall apart with age." "You're not giving up your love life, are you?" "What a man . . . You've lost all your old purity. Why have you become a man who says that kind of nasty thing? You used to be beautiful." Tabé, taking Kin's silver pipe, tried sucking on it. The bitter nicotine came out on his tongue. Taking out a handkerchief, Tabé spat the nicotine into it. "I haven't cleaned it, so it's clogged." Kin, smilingly, took up the pipe and shook it with short, sharp motions over a piece of scrap paper. Kin led a strange life, Tabé thought. The harsh times had not left a single mark on her. Her mode of life was such that it would probably be easy for her to raise two or three hundred thousand. Tabé had no lingering desire for Kin's body, but he felt as if he were closing in on the abundance of life in the woman that lay at the bottom of her existence. Coming back from the war, he'd gone into business with his usual energy, but within half a year he'd completely used up the capital from his brother. He was involved with a woman besides his wife, and had gotten her pregnant too. Remembering the Kin of old, he had come here thinking they might take up where they'd left off. But Kin was not the wholehearted lover she had been. He was unpleasantly aware of the gap between them. Even meeting him again after so long had inspired her with none of the old feeling. It was difficult to get close to this woman with her well-kept figure and disciplined face. Once more, he tried taking Kin's hand and holding it tight. Kin just let him do it. Not leaning over the brazier toward him, with the other hand she shook the nicotine from the pipe.

The long exposure to the months and years of absence had developed complicated emotions in both of them. The two had aged in parallel, so that the sweetness of the past would not come again. Silently, the two compared their present lives. They had sunk into the round of disillusionment. In complicated fatigue, they had come together. In this reality, there was none of the "chance" of a story. A novelistic coincidence might have been far more palatable. This was a gritty fact of life. The two had only met in order to deny each other. Tabé even had the fantasy of murdering Kin. But he had the curious feeling that to murder even this woman would be a crime. Though thinking what would it matter if he killed one or two women like this whom nobody cared about, when he thought that by doing so he would become a criminal, it seemed foolish and not worth it. Although she was an old woman who counted for nothing, here she lived her life, undisturbed by anything. In her two clothes chests, the wardrobe she had built up over fifty years must be compactly stored away. Tabé had been shown the bracelet given to her long ago by a Frenchman called Michel or something. She must have that kind of jewelry around. He knew for sure that this house belonged to her. His fantasy working strongly, he thought it would be no big deal to murder a woman with only a deaf-mute maid. But the memory of his student days when, in love with this woman, he had gone on seeing her through the worst of the war, came back with painful freshness. Whether it was because he was drunk, the ghost of the

Kin who sat before him was weirdly frozen inside his skin. He did not even want to touch her hand, but his past with Kin cast a thick shadow over his heart.

Getting to her feet, Kin went to the clothes closet and brought back a photograph of Tabé in his school days. "Hey, this is a funny thing to have." "Yes, it was at Sumiko's place. She let me have it. It's from before you met me. You looked like a young prince then. In your blue kimono with the white splash pattern. Please take it. You can show it to your wife. You're beautiful here. You don't look like a person who would say nasty things." "So I looked like this once, did I?" "You did. If you'd just gone on from there, you would have been a fine person." "You're saying I didn't turn out well, then?" "Yes, I am." "That's thanks to you, and the long war." "Ah, that's an excuse. Things like that are not the reason. You've become completely vulgar . . ." "So what if I'm vulgar? That's how people are." "And yet, wasn't I good to carry this photograph around for so long?" "You probably had some memories. You didn't give me one?" "Of myself?" "Yeah." "I'm frightened of photographs. But I must have sent you one of my geisha photographs when you were at the front." "I lost it somewhere." "See what I mean? I was much purer than you."

The "fortification" of the brazier between himself and Kin did not seem about to collapse. Tabé was already completely drunk. Kin's glass still had more than half the first drink in it. Gulping down the cold tea, Tabé put the photograph aside as a thing of no interest. "Are the trolleys still running?" "I can't go back now. You're not going to kick me out drunk like this?" "Yes, I'm going to throw you right out. This is a woman's house, and the neighbors would talk." "The neighbors? I didn't think you cared about such things." "I do care." "Is your lord and master coming?" "My! Nasty little Tabé-san. I'm shocked at you. What a hateful thing to say." "Forget it. Since I didn't get any money, I can't go back for two or three days. How about putting me up?" Kin, both cheeks propped on her palms, her large eyes widening, stared at Tabé's whitish lips. Even the love of a hundred years faded away. Silently, she scrutinized the man before her. The colors of the heart, of days gone by, had already vanished between them. There was none of the manly shyness of his youth. She felt like giving him a wrapped money-gift and making him leave. And yet Kin was averse to giving even a cent to this sloppy-drunk man. It was much better to give to an innocent, naive man. There was nothing so disagreeable as a man without self-respect. Kin had several times experienced the innocence of a man that made her crazy for him. She was drawn by such innocence, and she even thought it a noble thing. She had no interest in settling for a man without ideals. In her heart, Kin thought Tabé a trivial, degraded man. His luck, which had brought him back alive from the battlefield, made her feel the strength of fate. The hardships of having followed Tabé to Hiroshima alone ought to have rung the curtain down on this man. "What are you staring at a man's face for?" "But you were staring at me before. You were thinking of something not very nice, weren't you?" "No, I was all infatuated. I was thinking how each time I meet her, it's beautiful Kin-san." "Oh? Same here. What a splendid fellow Tabé-san's become, I thought . . ." "That's ironic." Tabé, not letting it slip out of him that he'd been thinking of killing Kin, got away with "That's ironic." "You have your prime ahead of you. It should be enjoyable." "You've still got some fun coming to you, no?" "Me? It's already over for me. I'll just go to seed from now on. In two or three years, I think I'd like to live in the country." "You mean it was a lie when you said you were going to live a long time, until you fell apart?" "I'm not saying that. I'm a woman who lives in her memories. But that's all. Let's be good friends." "No thanks. You're talking like a schoolgirl. I don't give a damn about memories." "That may be so . . . but it was you who talked about going to Shibamata." Tabé's knees were jiggling restlessly again. He wanted money. Money. He wanted to get something somehow out of Kin, even fifty thousand. "Are you sure you can't work it? Even if I put up my showroom for collateral?" "What? Back on money again? It's no good talking to me like that. I don't have a cent. I don't know anyone with that kind of money, and even if I seem rich I'm not. I need to borrow from you . . ." "Well, if it goes well, I'll bring you lots of money. Because you're an unforgettable person . . ." "That's enough of your soft soap . . . Didn't you say you weren't going to talk about money?" Suddenly the watery night wind of autumn blew in from all sides of the house. Tabé took up the tongs of the brazier. For a moment, the skin between his eyebrows crawled with terrible anger. A shadow, toward which he was drawn as by a riddle, made him grip the tongs hard. A throbbing that was like lightning hit his pulse. He was stirred up by that pulse. Kin, with uncertain, uneasy eyes, stared at his hands. She felt as if she were looking at a double exposure, as if the scene had taken place before in her life. "You've had too much to drink. It's all right if you stay the night." Tabé, told that he could stay, abruptly drew back the hand holding the tongs. Absolutely drunk, he staggered off to the privy. Kin, getting a presentiment from the look of Tabé from behind, laughed contemptuously to herself. People's feelings had changed utterly because of this war. Taking a philopon drop from the tea shelf, she quickly drank it down. There was still a third of the whiskey left. She would make him drink it, so he would sleep like mud, and send him away tomorrow. She alone could not sleep. On the blue flames of the well-kindled fire in the brazier, she burnt the photograph of the youthful Tabé. The smoke rose up thickly. A smell of burning hovered in the room. From the door she'd softly slid open, the maid Kinu peered inside. Kin, smiling, with hand signs told her to lay out bedding in the guest room. To get rid of the smell of burning paper, she put a piece of thinly sliced cheese on the fire. "Hey. What are you burning?" Tabé, back from the privy, his hand on the full shoulder of the maid, peered into the room. "I was wondering how cheese would taste if you burnt it. I was holding it in the tongs and dropped it." In the white smoke, a line of black smoke went straight up. The round glass shade of the electric light looked like a moon floating among clouds. The smell of burning oil was pungent. Kin, stifling from the smoke, went around the room roughly sliding open all the doors.

DAZAI OSAMU

[1909–1948]

Memories

At dusk, I was standing in the gateway with my aunt. She must have had a baby on her back, because she was wearing a nursery coat. I have never forgotten the dim quietness of the street at that hour. Our Lord has hidden Himself, my aunt told me, adding: "He was a living god." After that, I must have said something disrespectful. My aunt upbraided me, saying you mustn't say that sort of thing, you must say: "He has hidden Himself." "Where did He hide Himself," I asked purposely, although I knew where. I remember it made my aunt laugh.

I was born in the summer of 1909, so at the time of the Emperor's demise, I was a little over four years old by the Japanese count.* It was about the same time, I think, that my aunt took me on a visit to the house of relatives in a village about five miles from ours. I've not forgotten the waterfall I saw there. It was on a mountain near the village. From a green, moss-grown cliff, a broad cascade plunged whitely. Piggyback on the shoulders of a strange man, I gazed at it. There was a shrine on the bank there, and the man showed me the votive pictures of horses inside. But I felt more and more lonely,

---

*By which a fraction of a year is counted as one full year. (tr. note)

and after a while burst out crying. I screamed for my aunt. My aunt, with the relatives in a distant hollow where they'd laid down a carpet, was enjoying herself. At the sound of my crying voice she quickly stood up. She must have got her feet caught in the carpet, because she then staggered as if she were making a deep bow. Seeing that, the others made fun of her, saying she was drunk. Looking down on this from far up the mountain, I felt a rage of frustration and bawled and squalled louder than ever. Then one night, I dreamed my aunt had abandoned me and was leaving the house. Her breasts were stuck fast in the side door of the entryway. From those big, redly swollen breasts, beads of sweat dripped. My aunt was harshly muttering: "I don't like you anymore." Placing my cheek against the breasts of my aunt, I begged her not to go. My tears flowed. When my aunt shook me awake, I pressed my face into her bosom in the bed and cried. Even when I was awake, I still felt heartbroken and sobbed and sniffled a long time. But I did not tell my aunt or anyone else about the dream.

Although I have various memories of my aunt, unfortunately I don't happen to have any recollection of my mother and father at the time. We were a large household—my great-grandmother, grandmother, father, mother, three elder brothers, four older sisters, one younger brother, my aunt, and her four daughters—but it would be true to say that except for my aunt, until the age of five or six, I knew almost nothing of the others. In the spacious garden, there were five or six big apple trees, and I remember one dark, cloudy day when a lot of girls were climbing up into them. In a corner of that same garden there was a chrysanthemum bed, and once when it was raining I and the same crowd of girls, sharing umbrellas, gazed at the chrysanthemums in full bloom. These are only dim memories, but perhaps those girls were my sisters and cousins.

When I come to the age of six or seven, my memories also come clear. I was being taught to read by a maid called Také, and together we read all kinds of books. Také was devoted to my education. A sickly child, I read many books in bed. If there were no more books, Také would borrow armfuls of children's books from places like the village Sunday school. Learning how to read silently, I read any number of books without getting tired. Také also instructed me in morals. Often taking me to the temple, she showed me the hanging scrolls of Heaven and Hell and explained them to me. Those who had set fires carried on their backs baskets full of red, flickering flames; those who had had concubines choked in the coils of a blue, two-headed serpent. In the Lake of Blood, on the Mountain of Needles, in the bottomless deep hole called The Limitless Hell where white smoke hovered, everywhere, pallid, emaciated people opened their mouths in tight little *o*'s and wept and howled. If I told a lie, Také said, I would go to Hell and have my tongue torn out like that for the demons to eat. I burst into a storm of tears.

On a small slope in back of the temple, there was a cemetery. Along a hedge of yellow roses or the like, many tall wooden funerary tablets stood like a forest. A black iron wheel, the size of a full moon, was attached to the tablets. If you spun the wheel clatter-clatter, and when it stopped it stayed there without moving, the person who had spun it would go to Heaven. But if, once it had stopped, it then turned backward, the person would fall into Hell, Také said. When Také spun it, the wheel would spin around for a while with a nice sound and always quietly come to a full stop. But when I spun it, it now and then went backward. I remember one day, it was autumn I think, when I went to the temple by myself. No matter which of the wheels I tried spinning, they all, as if by previous arrangement, went backward with a heavy clatter. Keeping down my anger which was starting to explode, I stubbornly kept on spinning a wheel many tens of times. The sun had begun to set, so in despair I came away from that graveyard.

At that time, my mother and father were evidently living in To-kyo. Taken by my aunt, I went up to the capital. I'm told that I was there for quite a long time, but not too much of it remains in my memory. All I remember is the old lady who now and then came to visit that house in Tokyo. I didn't like this old lady, and every time she came I cried. Once she gave me a red toy Post Office truck, but it didn't interest me at all.

In due course, I entered grade school in my hometown. With that, my memories change completely. At some point, Také was no longer there. She'd gone as a bride to some fishing village. Perhaps from a fear that I would follow her, she had left abruptly, without a word to me. The next year, was it, at the Bon Festival, Také came back for a visit, but she was somehow distant. She asked about my marks. I did not answer. Somebody, for me, told her. Také, merely saying, "Negligence is the great enemy," did not even particularly praise me.

At the same period, circumstances arose which were to separate me from my aunt as well. Before then, my aunt's second daughter had married and gone away, the third daughter had died, and the oldest daughter had married the adopted son of a dentist. My aunt, with this daughter and her husband and the youngest daughter, was setting up a branch family in a faraway town. I went with them. It was winter, so I was huddled in the corner of the sled with my aunt. Before the sled began to move, my third oldest brother, jeering "son-in-law, son-in-law," poked my buttocks through the canvas many times. Clenching my teeth, I endured this humiliation. Although I'd thought I would be taken in for good by my aunt, when it came time to enter school, I was sent back to my hometown.

After I entered school, I was no longer a child. On the grounds of the empty house in back of ours, all kinds of weeds flourished. There, on a lovely summer day, in that meadow, I was taught something oppressive and suffocating by my younger brother's maid. I was around eight, and the maid couldn't have been more than fourteen or fifteen. In my part of the country, clover is called "bokusa." The maid, telling my brother, who was three years younger than I, to go and find a four-leaf "bokusa," chased him away. Then, holding me tight, she rolled around in the grass. And after that, hiding in the storehouse or the wardrobe, we played with each other. My younger brother was really a nuisance. Once, left by himself outside the wardrobe, he started crying and so we were found out by my third eldest brother. Told by my younger brother, he opened the door of the wardrobe. The maid calmly explained to him that she'd dropped a coin in there.

I was constantly telling lies myself. At the time of the Doll Festival, when I was in second or third year of grade school, I told the teacher that my family had said to come back early to help put out the dolls. Not staying for even an hour of classes, I went home and, telling everyone that there was no school today on account of the annual Peach Festival, lent an unneeded hand in taking the dolls out of their boxes. Another thing was, I loved little birds' eggs. Sparrows' eggs I was always able to get plenty of by lifting up the roof-tiles of the storehouse. But the eggs of the cherry-picker and the crow did not roll down my roof. Those green, as if burning, eggs and those curiously mottled eggs I got from my classmates. In return, I gave them five or ten books at a time from my library. Wrapping my collection of eggs in cotton, I filled a drawer of my desk with them. One night, my third eldest brother, who'd evidently gotten wind of my secret transactions, asked me to lend him a book of Western fairy tales and some other book. I resented my brother's ill feeling. Having invested both books in eggs, I no longer had them. If I said I didn't have them, my brother would investigate their whereabouts. I answered that I was sure I had them. Let's look for them, I said. Carrying a lantern, I searched my own room, of course, and the entire house. My brother, walking behind me, said with a smile: "I bet you don't have them." "I have them," I doggedly insisted. I even crawled up on top of the cupboard in the kitchen. Finally, my brother said: "That's enough."

The compositions I wrote at school, too, were all lies out of whole cloth. I expended great efforts in them to make myself out as a docile, good boy. When I did so, I was always praised and applauded by everybody. I even plagiarized. One, called "My Younger Brother's Silhouette," which was celebrated by the teachers as a contemporary juvenile masterpiece, was a prizewinning essay that I'd lifted whole from some children's magazine. My teacher, having me make a clean copy of it with a writing brush, entered it in an exhibit. Later, when the fraud was uncovered by a book-loving student, I prayed for that student to die. Similarly, another one, called "An Autumn Evening," was commended by all the teachers. It ran as follows. I'd gotten a headache from studying, so going out on the veranda I looked across the garden. It was a beautiful moonlit evening, and many carp and goldfish were playing in the pond. As, half in a trance, I gazed at that quiet scenery of the garden, from the next room there was a burst of laughter from my mother and the others, and all of a sudden my headache was gone. In this literary sketch, there was not a bit of truth. The description of the garden, if I remember correctly, was taken from one of my older sisters' composition books. And more than that, I have absolutely no memory of studying hard enough to give myself a headache. I hated school, and consequently did not crack a textbook even once. I only read books for entertainment. My family, as long as I was reading a book, any book, thought I was studying.

However, when I told the truth in my compositions, the results were invariably unfavorable. Once, when I penned a complaint that my parents did not love me, I was called into the faculty room by my teacher and given a stern talking-to. Assigned the theme "If There Was a War," I wrote that I was more afraid of war than earthquakes, thunder, fire, and my old man, and that if one came I would head for the hills right away. On my way, I would invite the teacher, because the teacher was a human being and I was a human being and our fear of war was probably the same. This time I was examined by both the principal and my assistant teacher. I was asked with what feeling I had written that. I prevaricated, saying that I'd written half in jest. The assistant teacher wrote in his notebook "Curiosity." After that, he and I began to have a little talk. When you write that the teacher is a human being and you are a human being, do you mean that all human beings are the same? Hesitantly, I answered that I thought so. I tended to be slow-spoken. Asked by him, "If the principal and I are the same, why do our salaries differ?," I thought for a while. Then I said: "Isn't it because your jobs are different?" Putting on his steel-rimmed spectacles, the narrow-faced assistant teacher immediately took down my words. For some time, I'd had a liking for this teacher. Then, he asked me this sort of question: Are we teachers and your father the same? At a loss, I did not answer.

My father, an extremely busy man, was not in the house too often. Even when he was at home, he was not with his children. I feared this father. Although I wanted his fountain pen, I was unable to say so. After racking my brains in solitude, I came up with the following stratagem. One night, in bed and keeping my eyes closed, I pretended to be talking in my sleep. Fountain pen, fountain pen, I called in a low voice to my father in the next room where he was talking with a guest. Of course, my voice reached neither my father's ear nor his heart. When my younger brother and I were having fun in the big rice storehouse, stacked to the rafters with straw rice bags, my father loomed in the doorway. "Boys, get out, get out of there," he admonished us. Standing in the light from behind, the big figure of my father seemed as black as coal. Whenever I think of my funk at that moment, I get a bad feeling even now.

Toward my mother, also, I was unable to feel affection. Suckled on my aunt's milk, growing up at her bosom, I did not know my mother until my second or third year in grade school. It was something that two of the menservants had taught me, but one night my mother, who lay beside me, suspicious of the movement of my quilt, asked me what I was doing. Terribly flustered, I replied that my hip hurt and I was massaging it. If that's so, you should rub it instead of just beating it, my mother said sleepily. For a while, I rubbed and stroked my hip in silence. In my memories of my mother, there are many lonely things. Taking my elder brother's Western clothes out of the storehouse, I put them on and walked among the flowers in the back of the garden, humming a mournful, improvised melody with tears in my eyes. Thinking I would like to play with the student-houseboy in the family office in this getup, I sent a maid to call him. But the houseboy did not come. Clicking the tip of my shoe against the stems of the bamboo hedge, I waited for him. Finally growing impatient, with my hands jammed into the pockets of the trousers, I burst out crying. My mother, who saw me crying, for some reason stripped the suit off me and slapped my buttocks hard and repeatedly. I felt as if I'd been cut with a knife, I was so ashamed.

From an early age, I was interested in clothes. If a button was missing on a cuff, I would refuse to wear the shirt. I loved white flannel shirts. The neck of my underwear also had to be white. I took care to let an inch or two of the white edge show at the front of my neck. On the day of the night of the full moon, the village students all came to school wearing their best clothes. I also, every year, wore a flannel kimono with thick tea-colored stripes. In the narrow school corridor, I would try running with short, mincing steps, like a woman. So as not to have that kind of affectation observed by others, I practiced it in secret. The people at home said that among my brothers I was the worst looking. If they knew that such an ugly boy played the dandy, I thought, they would probably all laugh at me. I pretended instead to be indifferent to clothes, and in that, I think, I succeeded to a certain degree. I'm sure I appeared to everyone as dull and countrified. When I was seated in front of my dinner tray with my brothers, my mother and grandmother often commented gravely on my bad looks. Naturally, I felt mortified. I thought I was a good-looking young man. Going to the maids' room, I would fish for a compliment. Who is the best looking of me and my brothers? I would subtly ask. Usually the maids would answer that my eldest brother was the best looking and after that Osa-chan. My face reddening, I was slightly dissatisfied even with this. I wanted them to say that I was handsomer even than my eldest brother.

It was not just because of my looks that I displeased my grandmother and the others. There was my clumsiness. Because of my unskillful way of holding the chopsticks, I was castigated by my grandmother at every meal. When I bowed, my rear end stuck up in the air and was painful to look at, I was told. I was made to sit up straight in front of my grandmother and perform my obeisance again and again, but no matter how many times I did so my grandmother did not say "good."

My grandmother, also, was a formidable opponent. When the village theater opened, and the Sasagi Saburo troupe from Tokyo was playing there, I went to see it every single day. Since my father had built the theater, I was able to sit in a good seat for free. As soon as I got back from school, I would change into a soft, luxurious kimono. With a little pencil dangling from my sash on a fine silver chain, I ran to the theater. It was the first time in my life that I had known the thing called kabuki, and I was excited by it. Any number of times, even during the farce interludes, I shed tears. After the engagement ended, I rounded up my little brother and the children of relatives, set up a theater, and gave my own plays. I'd always liked doing this sort of thing. Gathering the menservants and maids, I would tell them tales of the old days or have magic-lantern or movie shows. This time I presented three plays: *Yamanaka Shikanosuke*, *House of the Dove*, and *High Jinks*. The story of Yamanaka Shikanosuke recruiting a retainer called Hayakawa Ayunosuke in a teahouse on the bank of a mountain river, I took from a children's magazine and turned into a script. I, your humble servant, am known as Yamanaka Shikanosuke—I worked hard to recast such lengthy phrases in the seven- and five-syllable meter of kabuki. "House of the Dove" was a long short story, which, no matter how many times I read it, always brought tears to my eyes. In it, there was a particularly affecting part that I touched up into a two-act play. *High Jinks* was something which the Sasagi troupe, all hands on stage, always danced after the final curtain, and I decided to dance like that myself. Rehearsing for five or six days, at last on *the* day, making the wide corridor outside the library the stage, I hung out a little draw curtain. I busied myself in such preparations from noon on, but then my grandmother snagged her chin on the wire of the curtain. What are you trying to do with this wire, strangle me? Stop behaving like riverbed beggar-players, she berated us. Despite that, I gathered ten or so of the menservants and maids that evening and gave my performance, but when I thought of my grandmother's words I felt heavy and blocked. Although I took the parts of Yamanaka Shikanosuke and the boy in *House of the Dove* and danced in *High Jinks*, I could not feel any enthusiasm, only an unbearable loneliness. Even after that, I gave performances now and again of such plays as *The*

Cattle Thief, *The House of the Plates*, and *The Armor of Virtue*, but my grandmother had something unpleasant to say each time.

I did not like my grandmother, but on nights when I could not sleep I felt grateful to her. From my third or fourth year in grade school, I suffered from insomnia. Even by two o'clock in the morning, three o'clock, I could not get to sleep. Often I cried in bed. Although I was taught various sleep-inducing methods by the people of the house—licking sugar before going to bed, counting a clock's tick-tocks, cooling my feet with water, putting silk-tree leaves under my pillow—none of them worked very well. A worrier, I would brood over things and work myself into a state and so be all the more unable to sleep. Once, furtively fiddling with my father's pince-nez, I broke the lens—snap—and my feelings of guilt kept me awake for several nights. Next door but one, there was a knick-knack shop that sold a small number of books and magazines. One day, I was looking at the frontispieces of women's magazines. Among them, there was a watercolor of a mermaid in yellow that I desired with all my soul. Thinking I would steal it, I cut it out but was then reprimanded by the young owner. "Osa-boy, Osa-boy." Noisily flinging the magazine on the floor, I ran home. This kind of failed attempt also kept me horribly awake. Again, in bed, I would be attacked for no reason by fears of a fire. When I thought about what would happen if this house caught on fire, sleep was completely out of the question. One night, when I went to the bathroom on my way to bed, in the pitch-dark family office across the hall and down, the houseboy was showing himself movies. On the opaque sliding paper door, in a flickeringly projected rectangle the size of a matchbox, a polar bear plunged into the sea from an ice-cliff. As I peeped at that, the feelings of the houseboy seemed unendurably sad to me. Even after I got in bed, the thought of that lonely little movie show made my heart race and thud unbearably. What with brooding over the houseboy's sad lot in life and what I should do if the film in the projector caught fire and the house went up in flames, I was unable to sleep for anxiety. It was nearly dawn before I dozed off. It was on nights like this that I felt grateful to my grandmother.

Putting me to bed at around eight, the maid was supposed to lie beside me until I fell asleep. But, feeling sorry for her, I would pretend to be asleep as soon as I was in bed. Aware that the maid was stealthily creeping away from me, I would pray earnestly for sleep to come. After tossing and turning until ten o'clock, I would start sobbing and get up. At that hour, everybody in the house had gone to bed. Only my grandmother was still up. With the old night-watchman, she would be sitting and talking at the big sunken hearth in the kitchen. In my thickly padded, oversize kimono, I would sit between them sulkily and listen to their conversation. They were always gossiping about people in the village. Late one night in autumn, as I was listening to their subdued chitchat, I heard in the distance the beat of the drums of the torch procession for driving away noxious insects. I have never forgotten how encouraged I felt when I heard that. Ah, so a lot of people are still up, I thought.

I have memories about other sounds. My eldest brother, at that time, was at the university in Tokyo. Each time he came home for vacation, he disseminated through the countryside the latest tastes in music and literature. My brother was studying drama. A one-act play he'd written, called *The Struggle*, was published in a local magazine and much praised by the young people of the village. When he'd finished it, he read it to his many younger brothers and sisters. We can't understand it, they all said as they listened, but I understood it. I even understood the poetry implicit in the curtain-closing line: "It will be a dark night." I thought that instead of *The Struggle* he should have called it *The Pine Tree*. Afterward, on a corner of the mistitled manuscript page, I wrote my opinion in a small hand. Probably my brother did not notice that, since he published the play without changing the title. He had a rather large record collection. My father, whenever he held a banquet or the like in the house, always called in geishas from a distant town. From the time when I was five or six, I can remember being embraced by those geishas. I remember their songs and dances, such as "Long, Long Ago" and "It Was a Tangerine Boat from Kinokuni." From them, I was intimate early on with Japanese music rather than the Western music of my brother's records. One night, when I was in bed, a sound of music came from my brother's room. Raising my head from the pillow, I listened intently. In the morning, I got up early and, going to my brother's room, tried playing this record and that. Finally I found it. That record, which had so excited me the previous evening that I could not sleep, was *Ranchō*.*

But I was closer to my second eldest brother than to my eldest brother. Graduating with honors from a Tokyo commercial school, my second eldest brother had simply come home and was working in the family bank. He, also, was treated coldly by the family. I'd heard my mother and grandmother say that the worst-looking child was myself and the next worst-looking one, my second eldest brother, and I thought that the cause of his unpopularity was his looks. I remember my second brother's muttered joke, as though he were half teasing me: We don't need any of that, do we, Osa? We just wanted to be born with a manly bearing. But I never once really thought that my brother was bad looking. I also thought that he had the best head among us brothers. This second brother drank every day and had quarrels with my grandmother. Every time that happened, I secretly hated my grandmother.

As for my third eldest brother, I disliked him and he disliked me. Various secrets of mine were known by this brother, and I always felt at a loss with him. Also, my third eldest brother and my younger brother, having similar features, were praised by everyone as beautiful boys. I had an unbearable feeling of being oppressed from above and below by this pair. When this brother went away to middle school in Tokyo, I felt liberated at last. My younger brother, being the youngest child, had a gentle face and was loved by both my mother and father. Always envying my younger brother, I sometimes beat him. Scolded by my mother, I held a grudge against her. I think this was when I was ten or eleven. At times when the lice were swarming like sprinkled pepper in the seams of my shirt and underwear, because my younger brother smiled a little at that, I literally

*A ballad-drama of a love-suicide, which method Dazai himself was to employ. (tr. note)

floored him. But then I would get worried and smear ointment on the bumps on his head.

I was dearly loved by my older sisters. My oldest sister died, my second sister married, and my two other sisters each went to girls' school in a different town. There was no train in our village, and to go to and from the town where there was one, around seven miles away, there was a carriage in summer and a sled in winter. During the spring thaws and the sleety rains of autumn, there was no other way but to walk. The sled made my sisters sick, so even in winter they walked. Each year, I would go out to meet them by the stack of lumber at the edge of the village. Even when the sun had set completely, the road was bright in the snowlight. By and by, from the shadow of the woods of the next village, the paper lanterns of my sisters would flicker into view. Oh-h, I would shout, and wave my hands at their homecoming.

My older sister's school was in a smaller town than that of my younger sister, and her souvenirs, compared to those of the latter, were always modest. Once, blushing and saying, "They didn't have anything," my older sister took out five or six bunches of firecrackers from a basket and gave them to me. It made me feel sad, as if my heart were being constricted. Of this sister also, it was constantly being said by the family that her looks were bad.

This sister, until she entered girls' school, had lived with my grandmother in the detached quarters. I always thought she was my grandmother's daughter. My grandmother died at about the time I graduated from grade school. When, at the ceremony of placing her in the coffin, I saw that small, numb body of my grandmother in a white kimono, I was afraid that this image would cling to my eyes for a long time to come.

Not too long after that, I graduated. My health was weak, so my family decided to let me attend upper grade school for just a year. When I was strong enough, my father said, he would put me in middle school. Even so, since schools in Tokyo like my brothers' would be bad for my health, it would be a school farther out in the country. Writing a composition about how I did not particularly want to go to middle school but that my health was weak, I forced the sympathy of my teachers.

At this time, my village was made part of a town system. The upper grade school, financed and built in cooperation with five or six nearby villages, was in a pine forest upwards of a mile away from my village. On account of illness, I was always taking off from school, but as the representative of our grade school I had to try to be the best even at this upper grade school attended by many honor students from the other villages. Yet even there, I never studied. My self-conceit, which told me I was about to become a middle school student, taught me a stingy disdain for a mere upper grade school. Generally, during classes, I drew cartoon serials. At recess, I would put on a narrator's singsong and explain them to my classmates. I accumulated four or five notebooks of such cartoons. Sitting at my desk with my cheek propped on my hand, I would spend the hour vaguely gazing at the scenery outside the window. My desk was right by the window. A squashed fly had stayed stuck on the glass pane for a long time. As the fly vaguely loomed large in a corner of my eye, it seemed like a pheasant or a turtledove. Any number of times I was startled by it. Fleeing instruction with the five or six students who liked me, I would sprawl out with them on the banks of a marsh at the back of the pine forest and talk about the girl students. Tucking up our kimonos, we would compare the sparse pubic hairs that had started to grow there, and goose each other.

That school was for boys and girls, and yet I had never approached a girl of my own accord. Because my desires were violent, I suppressed them with all my might. I'd also grown extremely timid with women. Before then, two or three girls had had crushes on me, but I always pretended not to know. Taking down an Imperial Fine Arts Museum Catalogue from my father's bookshelf, I would gaze with burning cheeks at the "white pictures" concealed in it. Or, often, I would make a pair of rabbits I'd raised copulate, my heart thumping as the male rabbit bunched up his back. By such means, I contained myself. Since I was vain, I did not tell anybody, even about that "massage." Reading in books about its harmful effects, I did all I could to stop it, but to no effect. Presently, thanks to walking every day to that distant school, my body became strong. Around my forehead, little pimples like millet grains came out. This also I was ashamed of. I smeared a pure red ointment on them. That year, my eldest brother got married, and on the night of the wedding my younger brother and I snuck up to the bride's room. The bride, sitting with her back to the doorway, was doing her hair. At one glimpse of her faintly white, smiling face reflected in the mirror, I dragged my brother away. She's not so much, I bluffed strenuously. The shame I felt about my forehead, red with ointment, made me react all the more that way.

Winter drawing near, I had to begin preparatory studies for middle school. Looking at magazine advertisements, I sent away to Tokyo for various reference books. But, simply lining them up in my bookcase, I didn't read a word of them. The school was in the largest town in the prefecture, and there were always two or three times more applicants than elsewhere. Now and then, I was invaded by fears of failure. At such times, even I studied. When I'd studied continuously for a week, the certainty came to me that I would pass. When I was studying, I did not go to bed until nearly midnight and got up most mornings at four. Keeping a maid called Tami at my side, I would have her make the fire and heat the tea. No matter how late she'd sat up, the next morning Tami always came to wake me at four. By my side, as I puzzled over supplementary questions about the arithmetical mouse and her offspring, Tami would quietly read a story. Later, Tami was replaced by a fat, old maid. Knowing this was at my mother's instigation, I frowned when I thought of the motive behind it.

The following spring, when the snow was still deep, my father died coughing blood in a Tokyo hospital. The local paper published his obituary in a special edition. More than at my father's death, I felt excitement at this kind of "sensation." Among the names of the bereaved family, my name also was in the newspaper. My father's body, laid out in a big coffin, returned home on a sled. With a big crowd of townsfolk, I went out almost to the next village to meet it.

By and by, from the shadow of the woods, the awnings of a long line of sleds, bathed in the moonlight, came gliding out. Gazing at them, I thought it was a beautiful scene.

The next day, the people of the house gathered in the family chapel where my father's coffin had been placed. When the lid of the coffin was removed, everyone lifted up their voices and wept. My father seemed to be asleep. The high bridge of his nose had turned dead pale. Incited by the weeping voices, I shed tears myself.

For that month, the household was as busy as if the house were on fire. Distracted by the commotion, I completely neglected my study for the entrance tests. On the end-of-term tests at the upper grade school, too, I made up answers almost at random. My marks were third best in the class or thereabouts, but it was clearly because of the teachers' deference toward my family. Already, by then, I was experiencing a loss in my powers of memory. Unless I had prepared my answer, I could not write anything on the test. This was the first time that had happened to me.

A Golden Picture

When I was a child, I did not have a very good nature. I tormented our maids. I hated for them to be slow, and so I especially tormented the slow ones. O-kei was a slow maid. Even when I had her peel an apple, while she was peeling it—what was she thinking of?—she would pause two or three times, and if I didn't call her sharply to attention each time she might have sat there in a daze forever, the apple in one hand, the knife in the other. I thought she must be simple. Often I would see her in the kitchen, just standing there sluggishly, not doing anything. Slightly ashamed of myself, child that I was, I would get strangely angry with her. "Hey. O-kei. The day is short." Sounding very adult, I would fling such unfair words at her that even now, when I think about them, it makes my spine turn cold. As if that wasn't enough, one time I summoned O-kei and made her cut out with a scissors, one by one, the figures of soldiers in a parade from my picture book. There were hundreds of them swarming about—soldiers on horseback, soldiers carrying flags, soldiers with guns over their shoulders. It took the clumsy O-kei from morning until dusk without having lunch to cut out barely thirty of them. Even so, she had done such things as clip off half of a general's mustache, or cut out enormously large, like bear's paws, the hands of the soldiers with guns. I bawled her out for each mistake. It was summer, and O-kei sweated. All of the cutouts were soaking wet from the sweat of her hand. Finally I flew into a rage and kicked her. Although I was sure that I'd only kicked her on the shoulder, O-kei put her hand to her right cheek and threw herself down on the floor in tears. Crying and crying, she said: "I have never had my face stepped on, not even by my parents. I will remember this all my life." Her words, moaned out brokenly, gave me a bad feeling, as well they might. And in other ways, almost as if it was the decree of heaven, I made life hard for O-kei. Even now, I am somewhat like that. I just cannot put up with foolish, stupid people.

The year before last, I was kicked out by my family. Within one night, I was penniless. Hanging around the red-light district, throwing myself on people's mercy, taking life one day at a time, I was just beginning to think I would be able to support myself by writing, when I got sick. By the kindness of others, I rented a cottage for the summer by the muddy sea in Funabashi of Chiba Prefecture. There, cooking for myself, I was able to recuperate. Fighting against the night sweats that left my pajamas wringing wet night after night, I nonetheless had to work. Every morning I would have nothing but a glass of cold milk. Only that gave me the feeling of being curiously alive and happy. My head, too, ached with an absolute fatigue. The sweet oleander, in bloom in a corner of the garden, I was only aware of as something like a flickering of flames.

Round about that time, a policeman showed up in my vestibule. A short, skinny man close to forty, he was taking the census. Minutely comparing my name in the register with my face behind its several days' growth of beard, he asked: "Oh—but aren't you the young master?" He spoke with a thick accent of my hometown. "Yes," I nonchalantly replied. "And you?"

The policeman smiled so hard that it must have hurt his thin face.

"Well. So it is you, after all. Perhaps you've forgotten me, but nearly twenty years ago I was a wagon-driver back home."

Not smiling at all, I answered:

"As you can see, I've come down in the world."

"Oh, no, not at all." Smiling even more happily, the policeman added: "Just write your short stories, and you'll be a big success."

I smiled bitterly.

"By the way," the policeman went on, lowering his voice a little, "O-kei is always talking about you."

"O-kei?" I did not understand right away.

"Yes, O-kei. You've probably forgotten her. She was a maid at your house——"

I remembered. "Ahhh," I unconsciously groaned. Sitting there on the platform of the entryway, I hung my head. One by one, all the bad things I had done to that slow-witted maid twenty years ago came back to me now clearly. I almost couldn't bear to sit still.

"Is she happy?" As I lifted my face to ask this impertinent question, I recall exactly that a craven smile, that of the criminal, the defendant, hovered about my lips.

"Yes, she's getting along fine." Replying so cheerfully and openly, the policeman wiped the sweat from his brow with a handkerchief. "You wouldn't mind, would you? The next time I'll bring her along, so she can pay her respects."

I jumped up, terror-struck. "No! No! I don't—that is——" Violently refusing him, I writhed in an indescribable agony of humiliation.

But the policeman was serene and cheerful.

"The children, you know, my oldest works at the railroad station here. After him, there's a boy, a girl, and another girl. That last one is eight years old and entered grade school this year. It's a relief. O-kei has worked very hard, too. I don't know what it is, but a woman who has learned her manners by serving in a wealthy family like yours, there's something different about her." Blushing slightly, with a smile, he went on: "It's all thanks to you. O-kei never stops talking about you. The next holiday, she'll certainly come and visit you." Suddenly serious, he ended: "I'll take my leave for today, then. Be well."

Three days after that, worrying more about money than my work, I was unable to stay indoors. Taking a bamboo walking-stick, I was about to go out to the beach, when the door of the entryway was rattled open. Outside, three people—the father and mother in light cotton kimonos, a girl in a red Western-style school uniform, stood in a row as pretty as a picture. It was the family of O-kei.

In an angry voice, so loud it startled even me, I barked:

"You've come, have you? I have to go out now, on business. I'm sorry, but please come another day."

O-kei had become a mellow, middle-aged housewife. The eight-year-old girl looked very much like O-kei when she had been a maid. Her slightly dull, clouded eyes gazed vaguely up at me. Sadly, before O-kei could say a word, I rushed out to the beach as if in flight. Slashing at the tops of the beach grasses and plants with my stick, slashing at them, not once turning around, with a jerky gait as if stamping upon the ground in rage at every step, I headed heedlessly in a straight line for the town down the beach. What did I do in the town? Just meaningless things, like looking at the posters outside the small movie-house, or staring into the show window of the dry goods store. I kept clicking my tongue in chagrin. Somewhere in my heart, I could hear a voice mutter: "You've lost, you've lost." Thinking this wouldn't do, giving myself a violent shake, I began walking again—for how long, thirty minutes?—and then started back to my house.

Coming out onto the beach, I stopped short. Well, look at this— up ahead of me, there was a picture of peace. O-kei, her husband, and child were tranquilly skimming stones into the sea with cries of laughter. Their voices reached all the way to me.

"He's very—" the policeman, giving a stone a good hard throw—"He's got a good head on his shoulders, hasn't he? He'll be famous soon."

"That's so, that's so." It was O-kei's high, triumphant-sounding voice. "Ever since he was a child, he was a strange one. Even to the servants, he was kind and considerate."

Standing there, I wept. My angry excitement, with the tears, melted away into a wonderful good feeling.

I have lost. This is a good thing. It would have been bad if I had not. Their victory will shed luster on my departure tomorrow.

The Garden Lantern

The more I say, the less people believe me. All of the people I meet are on their guard against me. When I go for a friendly visit, just wanting to see a human face, they greet me with a why-have-you-come expression. It's unbearable even to think about.

It's gotten so that I don't want to go anywhere anymore. Even when I go to the public bath right in our neighborhood, I always choose the evening. I don't want to be seen by anyone. But when it was the middle of summer, my light cotton kimono gleamed whitely in the dusk and I felt terribly conspicuous. I was so embarrassed I could have died. Yesterday and today it has been much cooler. Day by day, it's getting to be the season for wool clothes. I intend to change as soon as I can to a dark serge kimono. If things go on this way and the fall passes and winter and spring go by and the summer comes around again and I have to walk around in my yukata again, it will be too much for me. At least, by next summer I would like to be able to wear this yukata with the morning glory pattern without feeling afraid. I want to stroll among the crowds on festival days with a little makeup on. When I think of how happy I'll be then, my heart's already pounding with excitement.

I committed a theft. That's what it was. I don't think what I did was good. But—no, I'll tell it from the beginning. I'll tell it to God.

I don't trust people. If there are people who believe me, fine, let them.

I am the daughter and only child of a poor clog-maker. Yesterday evening I was sitting in the kitchen, cutting up scallions, when from the field behind our house I heard a little boy sadly calling for his big sister. He was starting to cry. I laid down the knife, and thought. If I had a little brother or a little sister who loved me that much and called to me with tears, my life might not have to be this lonely . . . In my eyes, smarting from the smell of the scallions, hot tears welled up and flowed. When I wiped the tears with the back of my hand, my eyes stung even more and the tears came flowing out one after the other. In the end, I didn't know what to do with myself.

The time when the hairdresser started spreading the rumor that that selfish girl had finally fallen for a man was after this year's cherry blossoms, when wild pinks and irises were starting to appear in the night stalls of festivals. But it was a pleasant time. When the sun went down, Mizuno-san would call for me. Before then, I would already be dressed and made up. Any number of times, I went in and out of the gate of our house. The neighbors, seeing me like that and saying, "Well, the clog-maker's Sakiko has gone man-crazy at last," slyly pointed at me and laughed and whispered among themselves. Afterward, even I knew that they had. My mother and father also must have had some idea of what was going on, but they could not say anything. It's partly because of our poverty that although I will be twenty-four this year I haven't left home as a bride or had a son-in-law adopted into the family, but there is also my mother's past. She was the mistress of a big landlord in this neighborhood. Although he was good to her, she forgot all about that and ran away to my father's place after they'd talked it over. Almost the minute she arrived she had me. The fact that I didn't take after the landlord or my father made the world a very cramped place for my mother. For a while there, she was treated like an outcast. Probably for the daughter of such a family, late marriage is in the cards. Of course, with my kind of looks, even if I'd been born into the wealthy aristocracy it might have been my fate just the same. And yet, I don't hold anything against my father. I don't hold anything against my mother either. I am my father's child. No matter what anyone says, I believe that. Both my father and my mother love me very much. And I love them, and pity them. My father and my mother are both weak people. Even toward me, their own child, they are a little timid. I think that everyone should be gentle and sympathetic with weak, hesitant people. I thought that for my parents I could endure any kind of painful loneliness. But after I got to know Mizuno-san, I did neglect my duty as a daughter somewhat.

I am ashamed even to say this. Mizuno-san is a business school student who is five years younger than myself. But please forgive me. There was nothing else I could do. I met Mizuno-san this spring, in the waiting room of the hospital where I'd gone for an oculist when I had something wrong with my left eye. I am the sort of person who can like someone else at a glance. With a white bandage over his left eye the same as myself, and thumbing through a pocket dictionary with his brows knit as if he was displeased, Mizuno-san went straight to my heart. I too, on account of my bandage, was feeling gloomy and down in the dumps. Even when I looked out the window at the new leaves of the oak outside, they seemed to flare up in green flames, enfolded in a fierce heat-shimmer. Everything in the outside world seemed to be in a distant fairyland. Surely it was the sorcery of my bandage, too, that made Mizuno-san's face appear so beautiful, so precious, so otherworldly.

Mizuno-san is an orphan. He has no one to give him the love that comes from family. Originally his people were well-to-do drug wholesalers. But his mother died when Mizuno-san was a baby, and his father died when he was twelve. After that, the family broke up. His two older brothers and his older sister were taken in by scattered distant relatives. Mizuno-san, the youngest child, was brought up by a clerk of the shop. Now, although he is being sent to business school, he seems to have a very lonely life of it. He feels out of place in life. He told me himself, and he really seemed to mean it, that the only time he enjoyed himself was when he was out walking with me. He seems to lack all sorts of things in his life. This summer, he said, he'd made a promise with a friend to go swimming at the seashore. But he didn't seem to look forward to it; in fact he was all downcast about it. That evening, I committed a theft. I stole a pair of men's swim-trunks.

I sneaked into the Big Circle store, the biggest of its kind in our neighborhood. Making believe I was selecting some women's light summer wear, on the sly I reached for a pair of black swim-trunks in back. Tucking it neatly out of sight under my arm, I quietly left the store. I hadn't gotten more than twenty feet away when a voice yelled behind me: "Hey! You!" Feeling such terror that I wanted to scream, I began to run like crazy. Behind me the voice, deep and sonorous, shouted: "Thief!" Then I was struck on the shoulder so hard that I staggered. When I turned around, I was slapped hard on the cheek.

I was taken to the police station. In front, a dark mass of onlookers had gathered. They were all neighborhood people whom I knew by sight. My hair was all undone, and my yukata was pulled up exposing even my knees. A fine sight you are, I thought.

The policeman, sitting me down in a small room with a tatami mat at the back of the station, interrogated me. He was a pale, thin-faced unpleasant man of twenty-seven or -eight with gold-rimmed glasses. After carefully writing down my name, address, and age in a notebook, he suddenly grinned and said:

"How many times is this for you?"

I felt a chill of shock. I could not think of anything to say. As I hesitated, I thought: I'll be charged with a serious crime and put in jail. I have to talk my way out of this somehow. Desperate, I groped for the words of an explanation. But what was I to say? It was like being lost in an enormous fog. I have never been so frightened in my life. The words that I finally almost shouted out were clumsy and abrupt, but once I'd started I couldn't stop. I went on chattering away as if possessed by a fox. Somehow I felt as if I'd gone mad.

"You mustn't put me in jail. I am not a bad person. I am twenty-four years old. For twenty-four years, I have been a good daughter. I have done everything I could for my father and mother. How am I bad? I have never been talked about behind my back. Mizuno-san is a fine person. He's a man who is sure to make something of himself soon. I know he will. I didn't want him to feel ashamed. He'd made a promise to go to the seashore with a friend. I thought I'd give him what he needs to go to the beach. Why is that so bad? I am a fool. Yes, I'm a fool, but I'll show you—I'll give Mizuno-san a fine send-off. That person comes from a good family. He's different from other people. It doesn't matter what happens to me. If only that person gets a good start in life, I won't mind. I have my work. You mustn't put me in jail. I have never done anything wrong. Haven't I always taken good care of my poor parents? It's not fair. It's not fair. You mustn't put me in jail. You have no call to put me in jail. I've worked as hard as I can all my life, for twenty-four years, and now, because just for a minute I moved my hand the wrong way, just for that, you're going to ruin twenty-four years, no, my whole life? You mustn't. It's wrong. I just don't understand. Just because once in my life my right hand moved about a foot in spite of myself, does that mean I'm a kleptomaniac? It's too much. It's too much. Wasn't it something that happened just once, for two or three minutes? I am still a young woman. I have my life before me. I shall go on, living this hard life of poverty the same as I have up to now. Nothing else has happened. I haven't changed at all. I am the same person I was yesterday. What's one bathing suit to Mr. Big Circle? Aren't there people who cheat others, wring their money out of them, and then spend it all and get admired by everyone? Who exactly are the jails for? Only people with no money are put in jail. I can sympathize with thieves. They must be weak, honest people who don't know how to cheat others. Because they're not clever enough to make a good living cheating others, they slowly get driven into a corner. Then they do something foolish, like stealing a little money, and they have to go to jail for five or ten years. Ha ha ha! It's really funny. It's ridiculous."

I certainly must have been out of my mind. There's no doubt about that. Going pale, the policeman stared at me. All of a sudden, I thought I liked that policeman. Even though I was crying, I made myself smile at him. After that, I was treated like a mental patient.

Gingerly, as if touching a boil, the policeman conducted me to head-quarters. That night, I was detained in a cell. In the morning, my father came for me and I was allowed to go home. On the way, my father quietly asked me if I'd been beaten. That was all, he didn't say anything else.

When I looked at that day's evening newspaper, I blushed right back to my ears. There was a story about me. "Even a Shoplifter Has Her Reasons," the headline read. "Flowery Speeches from Eccentric Young Communist." The shame and disgrace of it all were not just that. The people of the neighborhood kept walking by and loitering in front of our house. At first I didn't know what it meant, but when I realized that they'd come to get a look at me, I trembled all over. It slowly came to me what a big incident that little act of mine had been. If there had been any poison in the house, I would have drunk it then. If there had been a bamboo grove near the house, I would have calmly walked into it and hanged myself. For two or three days, we closed the shop in the house.

Not long after, I even got a letter from Mizuno-san.

There is no person in this world who believes in you more than I. But your upbringing has been deficient. Although you are an honest young woman, there are bad things in your environment. I have done my best to correct your defects, but there was no changing them after all. People must have education. A few days ago, I went with a friend for some sea-bathing. On the beach, we had a long discussion about the necessity of ideals and aspirations for people. We are likely to make our mark in the world, and soon. You, too, Sakiko, must henceforth be humble in your behavior. To atone for even one ten-thousandth part of the crime you have committed, you must apologize deeply to society. Society hates the crime; it does not hate the criminal. Mizuno Saburo. P.S. Destroy this letter without fail after reading. Even burn the envelope. Without fail.

This was his letter in its entirety. I'd forgotten that Mizuno-san, after all, was the son of a rich man.

One by one, days that were like sitting on a mat of needles passed and already the cool weather's here. Tonight, my father, saying it was depressing with such a dim light bulb, changed the bulb in the six-mat room for a brighter one. And then the three of us, parents and child, ate our supper under the bright light bulb. My mother, saying, "It's dazzling, it's dazzling," shielded her eyes with the hand that held her chopsticks. She was in a buoyant mood. I poured the sake for my father. I told myself that for people like us happiness is in things like the changing of a light bulb, but somehow it didn't feel that lonely. Instead, it seemed to me that this house of ours, with its modest illumination, was like a very lovely garden lantern. If you look, see it! We three are beautiful, I thought. A quiet happiness, which wanted to tell it even to the insects singing in the garden, welled up in my heart.

Chiyojo

Women, after all, are no good. Even among women, I may be the worst of all. I don't know, but I think very badly of myself. Even as I say that, in a corner of my heart something stubborn that trusts in itself, that says there is one good thing in me somewhere, darkly and firmly coils its roots. More and more, I don't understand. Now I feel something absolutely oppressive and unbearable, as if my head was stuck in a rusty pot. Truly, my head's not right. It really is not. Already, next year, I will be nineteen years old. I am no longer a child.

When I was twelve years old, my uncle in Kashiwagi sent a composition of mine to the *Blue Bird* magazine. It won first prize, and the famous teacher who was the judge praised me so much it frightened me. Since then, I have gone to the bad. I feel ashamed of that composition. Was that kind of thing really any good? What was good about it, and how? The composition was entitled "The Errand," but it was a very slight thing about when I went to buy some Bat cigarettes for my father. I was given five packs of Bats by the old woman at the tobacco shop, but they were all green ones, and seemed lonely. So I changed one for a vermilion pack, and then I didn't have enough money. The old woman smiled and said, you can pay me later. It made me happy. Placing the one vermilion pack on top of the green ones, when I balanced them all on my palm they were as beautiful as a primrose. My heart began to palpitate, and I could hardly walk. That was what I wrote about, but now, when I think about it, the piece seems awfully childish and sentimental. It irritates me. Soon after, again at the urging of my Kashiwagi uncle, I submitted a composition entitled "Kasuga-cho." This time it was published not in the contributors' column, but on the very first page of the magazine in large type. What that "Kasuga-cho" was about was this. My aunt in Ikebukuro had moved to a neighborhood called Kasuga-cho in Nerima. I was told by her that there was a big garden and I must come out and see her. The first Sunday in June, I took the municipal railway from Komagoma Station, changing at Ikebukuro for a westbound line and getting off at Nerima. But everywhere I looked, there were only fields. I couldn't tell where Kasuga-cho was, and even when I asked some people in the fields they said they didn't know of such a place. I was ready to cry. It was a hot day. Finally, I asked a man of about forty who was walking along pulling a bicycle-cart full of empty cider bottles. Giving me a lonely smile, the man stopped and wiped the sweat that streamed down his face with a mouse-gray dirty towel. "Kasuga-cho, Kasuga-cho," he muttered to himself several times. Then he said: "Kasuga-cho is very far away. From the Nerima Station over there you have to take the eastbound line to Ikebukuro. There you change to the municipal railway. When you get to Shinjuku, you change to the inbound Tokyo line and get off at a place called Suidobashi." This terribly long itinerary, which he painstakingly explained to me in broken Japanese, seemed to be the way to get to the Kasuga-cho in Hongo. Listening to the man, I could tell right away that he was a Korean, but I was all the more grateful because of that. My heart became full. A Japanese person, even though he knows, thinks it's too much bother and pretends not to know, but this Korean man, even though he didn't know and the sweat was pouring down his face, did his honest best to try and tell me the way. "Thank you, thank you, sir," I said. And then, as the man had told me, I went to Nerima Station, changed back to the city-bound line and came home. I even thought of going as far as that Kasuga-cho in Hongo. After I got home, somehow I felt sad and out of sorts. So I wrote down everything just as it had happened. And it was printed in large type on the front page of the magazine. It became a big thing. My family lives in Nakazato-cho of Takino-gawa. My father is a Tokyo-ite, but my mother comes from Isé. My father teaches English at a private college. I don't have any older brothers or sisters. All I have is a younger brother who's in weak health. This year, my brother entered the municipal middle school. It's not at all that I dislike my family, and yet I am very lonely with them. Before, it was good. It was really good. I played the child with both my mother and father as much as I liked, played the fool all the time and made everybody laugh. I was very nice to my younger brother. I was a good older sister. But after that piece was published in the *Blue Bird*, I suddenly became a timid, unpleasant person. I even quarrelled with my own mother. When "Kasuga-cho" appeared in the magazine, in that same issue the judge, Mr. Iwami, contributed a description of his impressions that was two or three times longer than the piece itself. Reading it, I felt lonely. Mr. Iwami has been deceived by me, I thought. Mr. Iwami is a person of much greater beauty of feeling and simplicity than I am. After that, at school, my teacher Mr. Sawada brought the magazine to composition period and wrote out all of my piece on the blackboard. He was extremely excited. For a whole hour, as if giving me a stern talking-to, he praised me at the top of his voice. I began to be short of breath, and it got all misty and dark in front of my eyes. It was an awful feeling, as if my body was turning to stone. Because I knew that even if I was praised this much I was not worth it. I only worried about how painful it would be, how ashamed I would be when, after this, I wrote an inept composition and was laughed at by everyone. I didn't even want to go on living. And it wasn't as if Mr. Sawada was truly impressed by the piece. It was because it had been printed in a magazine in large type and praised by the famous Mr. Iwami that he got excited and said all those things. Even a child could more or less guess that that was why. And so I felt all the lonelier. It was unbearable. And everything I had feared came true in full. Only painful, shameful things happened. My friends at school abruptly gave me the cold shoulder. Even Ando-san, who up until then had been my best friend, abandoned me, calling me "Lady Murasaki" and "Miss Ichiyo" in a spiteful, derisive tone of voice.* Joining forces with Nara-san and Imai-san whom she had so disliked before, she would glance at me from far off and they would whisper together and then all at once burst into laughter and make coarse jokes. I will never write another composition in my life, I thought. I shouldn't have let my uncle in Kashiwagi talk me into submitting that piece. My uncle in Kashiwagi is my mother's younger brother. He works in the Yodobashi ward office. Although he will be thirty-four or -five this year and had a son born last year, he's still like a youth. Occasionally he drinks too much and makes a mess of things. Every time he comes to our house, he gets some money off my mother. When he was in college, he studied with the intention of becoming a writer and even though he was expected to by the upperclassmen, because of bad friends, he didn't. He even dropped out of school halfway through, I heard from my mother. He seems to have read an awful lot of short stories and novels, both Japanese and foreign. It was this uncle who, seven years ago, made me contribute that awkward composition to the *Blue Bird*. And it is this uncle who for the past seven years, in one way or another, has been egging me on to write. I didn't like books, then. Now it is different, but back then, when my silly compositions were published two straight times by the magazine, I was treated badly by my friends, the special treatment I got from my teacher was like a load on my back, and I really got to hate writing. After that, no matter how cleverly I was incited by my Kashiwagi uncle I never contributed anything anywhere. When he got on me too much about it, I would burst out crying in a loud voice. Even in composition period at school, not writing a line or a single word, I drew circles or triangles or a picture of a bride-doll's face in my notebook. Mr. Sawada, calling me into the faculty

*Higuchi Ichiyo, 1872–1896. (tr. note)

room, would scold me, saying I mustn't become conceited and must have self-respect. I felt mortified. But soon I graduated from grade school, and so was able to escape from that particular torment. When I began attending girls' school in Ochanomizu, there was not a single person in the class who knew about my banal prizewinning essays. It was a relief. During composition period, I wrote away happily and received average marks. Only my Kashiwagi uncle, always and annoyingly, kept pestering me. Every time he came to the house, he would bring three or four books of short stories and say: "Read them, read them." Even when I did read them, they were difficult and I didn't really understand them. Usually I would just pretend to have read them and hand them back to my uncle. Then, in my third year at girls' school, suddenly a long letter arrived for my father from that Mr. Iwami who was the judge of the *Blue Bird*. It seems to me that she has a precious talent, it began, or something like that, I just can't repeat the words, they make me so ashamed. But anyway, he somehow praised me very highly and said it would be a pity just to bury such a talent, won't you have her write a little something more, I will arrange for it to be published. He couched all of this in solemn, high-flown terms, far beyond anything I deserved. My father silently handed me the letter. Having him read it for me, I thought that this personage called Mr. Iwami was a truly serious, good teacher. But I could read quite clearly between the lines the officious handiwork of my Kashiwagi uncle. Approaching Mr. Iwami with some little stratagem, he'd contrived one way or another to make him write this letter to my father. There was no doubt about it. "Uncle asked him to do it. I know he did. Why is Uncle doing this kind of terrible thing?" Wanting to cry, I looked up at my father's face. My father, as if he also had seen through the whole thing, nodded slightly and said: "I don't think your uncle in Kashiwagi meant any harm by this. But I'm at a loss as to how to answer Mr. Iwami." He looked displeased. Apparently my father had never very much liked his younger brother-in-law. Even that time when I won the prize in composition, my mother and uncle were so happy they were beside themselves, but my father, saying this kind of over-excitement was bad for me, berated my uncle. My mother told me about it later, with a discontented air. My mother always says bad things about my uncle, and yet if my father says even a word against him she gets very angry. My mother is a gentle, lively, good person. But when it comes to my uncle, she occasionally has arguments with my father. My uncle is the demon of our household. Two or three days after I'd gotten that courteous letter from Mr. Iwami, my mother and father had a terrible quarrel at supper. "Mr. Iwami has spoken in such good faith," my father said. "To avoid rudeness on our part, I think I must take Kazuko to visit him and, explaining exactly how she feels, make an apology to him. It would be a pity if a misunderstanding arose and his feelings were hurt just on account of a letter." My mother, lowering her eyes, thought a moment. Then she said: "My brother is bad. He's really made trouble for everyone." Raising her face, she put up a stray hair with the little finger of her right hand and went on: "Perhaps it's our foolishness, but now that Kazuko has been praised by such a famous person, somehow I want her to do well in the future, too. If she has talent, I want her to develop it. You always scold her so, but aren't you being a bit obtuse yourself?" Speaking very fast, she smiled faintly. My father put down his chopsticks. "If you tried to develop it, it would do no good. A girl's literary talent is a very limited thing. A big fuss is made over a little flash in the pan, and the rest of her life is ruined because of it. Even Kazuko is afraid of that. The best life for a girl is to get married like everybody else and be a good mother. You people are trying to use her to satisfy your own vanity and ambition." He spoke in the manner of a teacher correcting a pupil. My mother, not even attempting to listen to his words, lifted and then set the earthen charcoal brazier at my side down with a thud. "Ahh! It's hot. I've burnt myself." Pressing the thumb and index finger of her right hand to her lips, with her face turned away, she said: "Even so, you know? It's not that my brother meant any harm by it." This time, my father put down both his chopsticks and his rice-bowl. "How many times must I say it before you understand? You people are trying to exploit Kazuko." Speaking in a loud voice, he lightly pushed his glasses back on his nose with his left hand and started to say something else when, suddenly, my mother burst out crying. Wiping her tears with her apron, she began to speak quite frankly about money matters such as my father's salary and the cost of our clothes. My father motioned with his chin to my brother and myself that we were to leave the room. Urging my brother, I withdrew to our study-room, but for an hour afterward I could hear the sound of fighting voices from the dining room. Usually my mother is a lighthearted and openhearted person, but when she gets in a rage she says things that are so brusque and brutal that one cannot listen to them. It was sad. The next day, on the way back from his school, my father went to Mr. Iwami's house both to thank him and to apologize. That morning, my father had asked me to go with him, but somehow I felt frightened. My lower lip was trembling, and I just didn't have the courage to go. My father got back around seven that evening. Mr. Iwami, he said, was a rather impressive person despite the fact that he was still a young man. He had been kindly sympathetic to my father's feelings, and had even offered his own apology. To tell the truth, he himself did not very much like to recommend a literary career to young women. Although he didn't come right out and say the name, he let it be understood that my uncle in Kashiwagi had asked him two or three times and so he'd had no choice but to write the letter. My father explained all this to my mother and me. When I gave my father's hand a pinch, my father softly closed his eyes behind his glasses and smiled. My mother, her demeanor calm as if she'd forgotten all about their quarrel, nodded acquiescently to everything my father said and did not say much of anything herself.

For some while after that, my uncle didn't show himself too often at our house. Even when he did, he was strangely distant with me and soon took his leave. I had completely forgotten about compositions. When I got home from school, I would work in the garden, run errands, help in the kitchen, help my brother with his homework, sew, do my own homework, or give my mother a massage. The busy days of being useful to everyone and full of energy went by.

Stormy weather was on its way. Unexpectedly, in January—this was when I was in fourth year of girls' school—my old grade school teacher, Mr. Sawada, paid us a New Year's visit. Both my parents, surprised and nostalgic, were very glad to see him, treating him as an honored guest. Mr. Sawada, however, had long since left the grade school and nowadays was doing odd jobs of private tutoring. He lived quite at loose ends, a carefree life, he said. But my feeling about him, although it is rude to say so, was that he didn't look carefree at all. Although he was about the same age as my uncle in Kashiwagi, he looked over forty or even near fifty. Even before, he had had an old face, but in these last four or five years that I hadn't seen him, he seemed to have aged twenty years and to be terribly tired. He didn't even have the strength to smile. It took a great effort. Hard wrinkles of pain folded his cheeks, and rather than feeling sorry for him I felt something unpleasant in him. His hair was cut short as always, but the gray hairs had increased noticeably. Unlike before, he only said very flattering things to me. I was flustered at first, and then it got painful to listen to him. Paying me transparent compliments about how good-looking I was and how well-mannered I was, he treated me with absurd politeness as if I were his superior. To my mother and father, he went on and on about my grade school days. He even brought up the matter of that composition which I had luckily managed to forget about. She has a very valuable talent, he said. In those days, I did not take too much interest in the compositions of schoolchildren. Also I did not know of a method to encourage the expression of the child's heart by means of the composition. Now, however, it is different. In regard to the compositions of schoolchildren, I have done sufficient research and, what is more, I have confidence in my method of teaching them. How would it be, Miss Kazuko, if, under my new guidance, you once more took up the study of composition? I promise results. And so on. Completely drunk, he gave out with this pretentious speech while leaning full-length on one elbow. At the end, he stubbornly insisted that I "shake the hand of friendship." My mother and father, while looking on with smiles, seemed privately dumbfounded. But what Mr. Sawada said that time when he was drunk turned out to be no random joke. About ten days afterward, with a meaningful look on his face, he came to the house again. Little by little, he said, we shall begin practicing the basics of composition. I didn't know what to do. This was something I heard later, but Mr. Sawada, because of some incident that had occurred during preparations for exams at his school, had been let go. After that, his life not going as he wished it to, he had been making the rounds of his former pupils' houses and forcing his impersonation of a private tutor on them for a sort of livelihood. Apparently not long after his New Year's visit, he had sent a letter to my mother on the sly, praising my literary talent to the skies, and citing as an example of what might be done with it the recent popularity of the schoolchild composition and the appearance of "girl geniuses." My mother had always felt regret that I hadn't gone on with my writing. She answered him that he could kindly come once a week and tutor me privately. To my father, she said that it was to help Mr. Sawada a little in making his living. My father, since Mr. Sawada was my old teacher and he could not say no, reluctantly let him come. Evidently those were the circumstances. From then on, Mr. Sawada came every Saturday. In my study-room, he would say the silliest things in a whispery sort of voice. It was just unbearable. He repeated over and over again, as if they were very important, such obvious points as that in writing the first thing was to make sure of one's prepositions. " 'Taro is playing on the garden' is wrong. 'Taro is playing at the garden' is wrong, too. You must say 'Taro is playing *in* the garden.' " When I giggled at this, he would gaze at me reproachfully and, breathing a deep sigh, say: "You are lacking in sincerity. No matter how much talent a person has, if he does not have sincerity, he will never succeed in anything. Do you know of Terada Masako, the literary girl genius? She was born in poverty, and even when she wished to study she could not buy a single book. That is how deprived and sad her life was. Yet she had what was needed, sincerity. She paid close attention to her teacher and, because of that, was able to write such a literary masterpiece. And how proud her teacher must have been, how well rewarded! If you had a little more sincerity, I could make you into another Terada

Masako, no, since you are blessed by comfortable circumstances I could make you into a greater writer than she. In one particular, I believe I am more advanced than Masako-san's teacher. That is the particular of moral training. Do you know of a person called Rousseau, Jean-Jacques Rousseau, he lived in the sixteen hundreds, no, the seventeen hundreds, the nineteen—laugh, yes, laugh your head off, you rely too much on your talent, you scorn instruction. In the olden days, in China, there was a man named Gankai," and so on. When this had gone on for an hour or so, he would calmly break off and, saying, "Until next week, then," leave my room and gossip a while with my mother in the tearoom before going home. It isn't nice to talk this way about a teacher to whom I do owe something from my grade school days, but really, I could only think that Mr. Sawada was getting senile. "In writing, description is the important thing. Unless you have description, nobody knows what you're writing about," etc. Saying overly obvious things like this, he'd glance at a little notebook. "For instance, when you describe how that snow is falling. . ." Putting away the notebook in a chest pocket of his jacket, he looked for a long moment at the fine snow that, as if in a play, was falling thickly outside the window. "You must not say 'The snow is falling heavily.' It does not give the feeling of the snow. Nor must you say 'It is falling rapidly.' How about 'It is falling flutteringly'? No, still not good enough. 'Flittering,' this is closer. Gradually we have gotten close to the feeling of the snow. This is interesting." Talking to himself and nodding his head, impressed by himself, he folded his arms and mumbled: "'Gently falling,' how's that? Or is that a description of spring rain? Shall we after all make it 'flittering'? It would be fun to join the two. Yes, that's it: 'Flitter-flitter, flutter-flutter. Flitter-flutter, flutter-flitter.'" Narrowing his eyes, he seemed to savor the aptness of the description. Then, suddenly: "No! Still not good enough. Ah—'The snow flies and scatters like goose-down.' The old writers had it right after all. 'Like goose-down'—that was well said . . . Kazuko-san, have you understood?" Only now did he turn and speak to me. Gradually my teacher had come to seem both pathetic and repulsive. I was ready to weep. But for three months or so I endured that kind of forlorn, slapdash coaching. Already, though, just to look at Mr. Sawada's face was an ordeal. Finally, I went to my father and told him everything. I begged him please not to let Mr. Sawada come anymore. My father, hearing me out, said: "This is extraordinary." From the start, my father had been against the idea of a tutor, but giving in to the pretext that it would help Mr. Sawada, he'd asked him to come. He never thought that it would mean this sort of irresponsible instruction in composition-writing. I think he just thought that Mr. Sawada would come once a week and help me a little with my homework. He immediately had a terrible argument with my mother. In my study-room, listening to them argue in the tearoom, I wept to my heart's content. I felt that with all the trouble I had caused I must be the worst, most disobedient daughter in the world. I thought that if it was going to be like this I would rather study composition and short stories as hard as I could and make my mother happy. But I am no good. Already, I can't write anything at all. I never had talent, or anything like it. Even in that description of the falling snow, Mr. Sawada was surely more skillful than I. Although I'm capable of nothing, I am such a fool of a girl that I was laughing at Mr. Sawada. I could never have thought even of a phrase like "flitter-flitter, flutter-flutter." As I listened to the quarrel in the tearoom, I thought: "Truly I am a bad girl."

This time, my mother gave in to my father and Mr. Sawada no longer showed his face at our house. But the bad things went on happening. In the Fukugawa section of Tokyo, an eighteen-year-old girl called Kanazawa Fumiko wrote a really splendid book that became the talk of the world. It was said that her book had sold far better than those of the most intellectual writers, and that she had leapt at a single bound into the ranks of the rich. My Kashiwagi uncle, coming to the house with such an expression of triumph you'd have thought he himself had become rich, told my mother about it. My mother, too, got excited and said Kazuko has the talent if she will only use it, why is she different from before, and although she's a woman, always hanging around the house, it won't do, and she should write something with a little help from you. At least my uncle, unlike Mr. Sawada, had got as far as college. Whatever one said, there was something promising about it, and even my father, if it was a question of that much money, would overlook it, said my mother, full of enthusiasm as she tidied up in the kitchen. From then on, my Kashiwagi uncle started coming to the house again, almost every day. Taking me into the study-room, he would say such things as, first of all, I should keep a diary, if I wrote down exactly what I had observed and what I had felt, that in itself would be very good writing. Then he would give me all sorts of complicated reasons, which, since I didn't have the least desire to write, I always let in one ear and out the other. My mother was the sort of person whose excitement soon dies down; this time also her enthusiasm lasted for about a month and then she was calm and unconcerned again. Only my Kashiwagi uncle, far from losing interest, said with a serious face that he was really and truly going to make a writer of me this time. "Kazuko, after all, is a woman who has no other choice than to be a writer. A girl with such a strange, good mind cannot just be an ordinary housewife. She must give up everything and purify herself on the road of art," etc. He would lecture my mother and me this way when my father was out of the house. My mother, as might be expected when she was talked at so loud and long, did not seem to get a good feeling from it. "Is that how it will be for her? Then shouldn't we feel sorry for Kazuko?" she would ask with a lonely smile.

Perhaps my uncle was right in what he said. The next year I graduated from girls' school and now, well now, while hating my uncle's devilish prediction so much I could die, in a corner of my heart is something that secretly acquiesces: it may be so. I am a botched woman. Certainly, my head is not right. I have become incomprehensible to myself. When I left girls' school, I suddenly became a different person. Day after day, I was bored. Helping around the house, taking care of the garden, practicing on the koto, doing things for my brother, anything—it all seemed foolish. Not letting my mother and father know, I did nothing but read stories about love affairs. Why do short stories tell nothing but the bad,

secret things about people? I've become an impure woman, who has
lewd fantasies. Now, indeed, I think I would like to do as my uncle
told me once and write down exactly what I've observed and felt and
apologize to God, but I don't have the courage. No, I don't have the
talent. All I have is this absolutely unbearable feeling, as if my head
were jammed inside a rusty pot. I cannot write anything. Of late,
I've even been thinking that I want to write. The other day, secretly,
as an exercise, I wrote down in my notebook a silly little story about
something that happened one night. I called it "The Sleeping Box."
I asked my uncle to read it. Whereupon my uncle, before he had
read even half of it, tossed the notebook aside and said with a sober,
disappointed face: "You've given up on the idea of being a writer,
haven't you, Kazuko. Probably just as well." Then, with a sour
smile, as if warning me off the idea, he told me that unless one had a
special talent for writing it was no good. Now, on the contrary, it's
my father who smiles at me casually and says that if I want to I may
write. Now and then my mother, hearing talk somewhere about
Kanazawa Fumiko or about how some other girl has become famous
overnight, comes home all excited and says Kazuko, you can write if
you only want to, you have no perseverance, that's bad. In the olden
days, when Chiyojo of Kaga went to a master to learn the art of haiku,
she was told first of all to write a poem about a nightingale. Right
away she composed several different poems, and showed them to her
teacher. But the master did not say that they were good. And so,
Chiyojo thought about it all one sleepless night. And then, she suddenly noticed it was dawn. And without especially thinking of it, she
wrote:

> The nightingale, the
> nightingale, it sings at dawn
> it sings at dawn o!

And when she showed it to her teacher, for the first time he praised
her, saying, "Chiyojo, you've done it!" Isn't that so? You've got to
have perseverance in everything, my mother says, and, taking a sip
of tea, murmurs the poem over to herself. That was well written, she

says, solitary in her admiration. Mother, I am not Chiyojo. I am a girl writer of low intelligence who can't write anything. I wrote one little story about how when I put my legs under the quilt of the sunken hearth and read a magazine, I grew sleepy and so I thought that the kotatsu was like a sleeping box for people. But when I showed it to my uncle, he tossed it away half unread. Afterward, when I tried to read it, sure enough it was of no interest. How am I to become a good writer? Yesterday, I secretly sent a letter to Mr. Iwami. Please don't forsake your "talented girl" of seven years ago, I wrote. I may go insane one of these days.

KOBO ABÉ
[1924–   ]

The Red Cocoon

The sun is starting to set. It's the time when people hurry home to their roosts, but I don't have a roost to go back to. I go on walking slowly down the narrow cleft between the houses. Although there are so many houses lined up along the streets, why is there not one house which is mine? I think, repeating the same question for the hundredth time.

When I take a piss against a telephone pole, sometimes there's a scrap of rope hanging down, and I want to hang myself. The rope, looking at my neck out of the corner of its eye, says: "Let's rest, brother." And I want to rest, too. But I can't rest. I'm not the rope's brother, and besides, I still can't understand why I don't have a house.

Every day, night comes. When night comes, you have to rest. Houses are to rest in. If that's so, it's not that I don't have a house, is it?

Suddenly, I get an idea. Maybe I've been making a serious mistake in my thinking. Maybe it's not that I don't have a house, but that I've forgotten it. That's right, it could be. For example, I stop in front of this house I happen to be passing. Might not this be my house? Of course, compared to other houses, it has no special feature

159

that particularly breathes out that possibility, but one could say the same of any house. That cannot be a proof canceling the fact that this may be my house. I'm feeling brave. OK, let's knock on the door.

I'm in luck. The smiling face of a woman looks out of a half-opened window. She seems kind. The wind of hope blows through the neighborhood of my heart. My heart becomes a flag that spreads out flat and flutters in the wind. I smile, too. Like a real gentleman, I say:

"Excuse me, but this isn't my house by any chance?"

The woman's face abruptly hardens. "What? Who are you?"

About to explain, all of a sudden I can't. I don't know what I should explain. How can I make her understand that it's not a question now of who I am? Getting a little desperate, I say:

"Well, if you think this isn't my house, will you please prove it to me?"

"My god . . ." The woman's face is frightened. That gets me angry.

"If you have no proof, it's all right for me to think it's mine."

"But this is my house."

"What does that matter? Just because you say it's yours doesn't mean it's not mine. That's so."

Instead of answering, the woman turns her face into a wall and shuts the window. That's the true form of a woman's smiling face. It's always this transformation that gives away the incomprehensible logic by which, because something belongs to someone, it does not belong to me.

But, why . . . why does everything belong to someone else and not to me? Even if it isn't mine, can't there be just one thing that doesn't belong to anyone?

Sometimes, I have delusions. That the concrete pipes on construction sites or in storage yards are my house. But they're already on the way to belonging to somebody. Because they become someone else's, they disappear without any reference to my wishes or interest in them. Or they turn into something that is clearly not my house.

Well then, how about park benches? They'd be fine, of course. If they were really my house, and if only he didn't come and chase me off them with his stick . . . Certainly they belong to everybody, not to anybody. But he says:

"Hey, you, get up. This bench belongs to everybody. It doesn't belong to anybody, least of all you. Come on, start moving. If you don't like it, you can spend the night in the basement lockup at the precinct house. If you stop anyplace else, no matter where, you'll be breaking the law."

The Wandering Jew—is that who I am?

The sun is setting. I keep walking.

A house . . . houses that don't disappear, turn into something else, that stand on the ground and don't move. Between them, the cleft that keeps changing, that doesn't have any one face that stays the same . . . the street. On rainy days, it's like a paint-loaded brush, on snowy days it becomes just the width of the tire ruts, on windy days it flows like a conveyor belt. I keep walking. I can't understand why I don't have a house, and so I can't even hang myself.

Hey, who's holding me around the ankle? If it's the rope for hanging, don't get so excited, don't be in such a hurry. But that's not what it is. It's a sticky silk thread. When I grab it and pull it, the end's in a split between the upper and sole of my shoe. It keeps getting longer and longer, slippery-like. This is weird. My curiosity makes me keep pulling it in. Then something even weirder happens. I'm slowly leaning over. I can't stand up at a right angle to the ground. Has the earth's axis tilted or the gravitational force changed direction?

A thud. My shoe drops off and hits the ground. I see what's happening. The earth's axis hasn't tilted, one of my legs has gotten shorter. As I pull at the thread, my leg rapidly gets shorter and shorter. Like the elbow of a frayed jacket unraveling, my leg's unwinding. The thread, like the fiber of a snake gourd, is my disintegrating leg.

I can't take one more step. I don't know what to do. I keep on standing. In my hand that doesn't know what to do either, my leg that has turned into a silk thread starts to move by itself. It crawls out smoothly. The tip, without any help from my hand, unwinds itself and like a snake starts wrapping itself around me. When my left leg's all unwound, the thread switches as natural as you please to my right leg. In a little while, the thread has wrapped my whole body in a bag. Even then, it doesn't stop but unwinds me from the hips to the chest, from the chest to the shoulders, and as it unwinds it strengthens the bag from inside. In the end, I'm gone.

Afterward, there remained a big empty cocoon.

Ah, now at last I can rest. The evening sun dyes the cocoon red. This, at least, is my house for sure, which nobody can keep me out of. The only trouble is now that I have a house, there's no "I" to return to it.

Inside the cocoon, time stopped. Outside, it was dark, but inside the cocoon it was always evening. Illumined from within, it glowed red with the colors of sunset. This outstanding peculiarity was bound to catch his sharp policeman's eye. He spotted me, the cocoon, lying between the rails of the crossing. At first he was angry, but soon changing his mind about this unusual find, he put me into his pocket. After tumbling around in there for a while, I was transferred to his son's toy box.

The Flood

A certain poor but honest philosopher, to study the laws of the universe, took a telescope up to the roof of his tenement and pursued the movements of the heavenly bodies. As always, he seemed unable to discover more than a few meaningless shooting stars and the stars in their usual positions. It was not that he was bored or anything, but he happened to turn his telescope casually on the earth. An upside-down road dangled in front of his nose. A similarly inverted worker appeared, walking backwards along the road. Righting these images in his head, and returning them to their usual relationship, the philosopher adjusted the lens and followed the worker's movements. Under the wide-bore lens, the interior of the worker's little head was transparent. The reason was that the worker, on his way back from the night shift at the factory, had nothing in his head but fatigue.

However, the persevering philosopher, not turning the lens aside because of that, continued to follow the worker's progress. The philosopher's patience was soon rewarded. Suddenly, the following changes took place in the worker.

The outline of the worker's body unexpectedly grew blurred. Melting from the feet up, the figure knelt slimily and dissolved.

Only the clothes, cap, and shoes remained, in a mass of fleshy liquid. Finally, completely fluid, it spread out flat on the ground.

The liquefied worker quietly began to flow toward lower ground. He flowed into a pothole. Then he crawled out of it. This movement of the liquid worker, in defiance of the laws of hydrodynamics, amazed the philosopher so much that he almost dropped the telescope. Flowing onward, the worker, when he came up against a roadside fence, crawled up it just like a snail gliding on its membrane, and disappeared from view over the fence. The philosopher, taking his eye from the telescope, heaved a deep sigh. The next day, he announced to the world the coming of a great flood.

Actually, everywhere in the world, the liquefaction of workers and poor people had begun. Particularly remarkable were the group liquefactions. In a large factory, the machinery would suddenly stop. The workers, deliquescing all at once, would form a single mass of liquid that flowed in a stream under the door or, crawling up the wall, flowed out the window. Sometimes the process was reversed: after the workers had turned into liquid, only the machinery, in the deserted factory, would senselessly continue running and in the end break down. In addition, breakouts from prisons due to the mass liquefaction of the prisoners and small floods caused by the liquefaction of whole populations of farm villages were reported one after another in the newspapers.

The liquefaction of human beings, not limited to this kind of phenomenal abnormality, occasioned confusion in a variety of ways. Perfect crimes owing to the liquefaction of the criminal increased dramatically. Law and order were threatened. The police, secretly mobilizing the physicists, began an investigation of the properties of this water. But the liquid, completely ignoring the scientific laws of fluids, merely plunged the physicists into ludicrous confusion. Although to the touch it was in no way different from ordinary water, at times it displayed a strong surface tension like mercury and could retain its shape like amoebae, so that not only could it crawl, as indicated before, from a low to a higher place, but after blending perfectly with its fellow liquefied people and other natural liquids, at some impulse or other it could also separate itself into its original volume. Again, conversely, it sometimes displayed a weak surface tension like that of alcohol. At such times, it had an extraordinary power of permeation vis-à-vis all solids. E.g., at times, probably in relation to differences in its use, with the same kind of paper it could either have absolutely no effect or could dissolve it chemically.

The liquefied human beings were also able to freeze or evaporate. Their freezing and evaporation points were various. Sleighs running over thick ice would be swallowed up horse and all by the suddenly melted ice; front-runners in skating contests would abruptly vanish. Again, swimming pools would suddenly freeze in midsummer, sealing up girls who'd been swimming in them in frozen poses in the ice. The liquid human beings crawled up mountains, mixed with rivers, crossed oceans, evaporated into clouds and fell as rain, so that they spread all over the world. One could never tell what kind of thing was going to happen when and where. Chemistry experiments became well-nigh impossible. The boilers of steam engines, because of an admixture of liquid people, became completely unserviceable. No matter how much they were stoked, no pressure built up. Or all of a sudden the liquid people would violently expand and explode the boiler. Fish and plants that had a vital relationship to water were in a state of chaos beyond description. In every field of biology, transformations difficult to calculate, and destructions, had begun. Apples rolled around warbling snatches of melody; rice-stalks burst with a noise like firecrackers. Especially serious were the effects on human beings who had not yet deliquesced, and in particular on rich people.

One morning, the owner of a big factory drowned in a cup of coffee as soon as he put his lips to the cup. Another industrialist drowned in a glass of whiskey. An extreme example was a drowning in a single drop of eyewash. These seem like things scarcely to be believed, but they all happened.

As these facts were reported, many rich people contracted hydrophobia in the true sense of the word. A certain high government official made the following confession: "When I'm about to drink, I look at the water in the glass and already it does not seem like water to me. In short, it is a liquidized mineral, a harmful substance that is impossible to digest. If I took a mouthful, I am positive I would immediately get sick. I'm instantly invaded by tragic fears."

Even if dysphagia were not present, this was plainly hydrophobia. Everywhere, there were instances of old ladies who fainted away at the mere sight of water. Yet antirabies vaccine did no good whatsoever.

By now, from one end of the world to the other, invisible voices were mingling in a chorus crying doom by a great flood. But the newspapers, at first publishing the following reasons, strenuously denied those rumors:

a) This year's rainfall, both regional and global, is below the annual average.

b) All rivers reported to have flooded have not exceeded the seasonal variation for a normal year.

c) No meteorological or geological abnormalities have been observed.

These were the facts. But it was also a fact that the flood had already started. This contradiction caused general social unrest. It was already clear to everyone that this was no ordinary flood. Presently even the newspapers were forced to acknowledge the reality of the flood. But in their usual optimistic tone, they reiterated that this was due to some cosmic accident, was no more than temporary, and would soon end of its own accord. However, the flood, spreading daily, engulfed many villages and towns, many flatlands and low hills were submerged by the liquid people, and the people of status, the people of wealth, began a competitive stampede for refuge in the uplands and mountain districts. Although realizing that that kind of thing was useless against the liquid people who climbed even walls, they were unable to think of anything else to do.

Finally, even the presidents and prime ministers admitted the urgency of the situation. Proclamations were issued, saying that in order to save humanity from extinction in this flood it was necessary to mobilize all spiritual and material resources and expedite the building of great dams and dikes. Tens of thousands of workers, for that purpose, were rounded up for compulsory labor. Whereupon the newspapers also, suddenly changing their attitude, chimed in with the proclamations and praised their high morality and sense of public duty. But just about everybody, including the presidents and prime ministers, knew that those proclamations were nothing more than proclamations for the sake of proclamations. Dikes and such, against the liquid people, being no more than Newtonian dynamics against quantum dynamics, were completely ineffectual. Not only that, but the workers constructing the dikes were rapidly turning into liquid this side of the dikes. The "personal items" pages of the newspapers were awash with notices of missing persons. But, true to character, the newspapers dealt with such disappearances simply as effects rather than causes of the flood. In regard to the contradictory nature of the flood and its essential cause, they maintained a resolute silence, refusing even to mention the subject.

At this time, there was a scientist who proposed that the liquid that had covered the earth be volatilized by means of nuclear energy. The governments, speedily indicating their approval, pledged their full-scale assistance. But when they tried to begin, what became clear, rather than various difficulties, was the impossibility of the project. Because of the liquefaction of human beings, which was accelerating at geometrical progression, there were not enough workers for adequate replacements. Also, liquefaction was already occurring among the scientists. Furthermore, the parts factories were steadily being destroyed and engulfed by the waters. Harassed by problems of reorganization and reconstruction, governments could not predict when the production of vital nuclear equipment would begin.

Unrest and distress swept the world. People were turning into mummies from dehydration, emitting gasping, rattling noises each time they breathed.

There was just one person who was calm and happy. This was the optimistic and wily Noah. Noah, from his experience with the previous flood, without getting agitated or panicky, diligently worked on his ark. When he thought that the future of the human race was being entrusted to him and his family alone, he was even able to steep himself in a religious exaltation.

Presently, when the flood approached his house, Noah, accompanied by his family and domestic animals, boarded the ark. Immediately, the liquid people started to crawl up the sides of the boat. Noah berated them in a loud voice.

"Hey! Whose boat do you think this is? I am Noah. This is Noah's Ark. Make no mistake about it. Go on, get out of here!"

But to think that the liquid, which was no longer human, could understand his words was clearly a hasty conclusion and a miscalculation. For liquid, there are only concerns of liquid. The next minute, the ark filled up with liquid and the living creatures drowned. The derelict ark drifted at the mercy of the wind.

In this manner, humanity perished in the Second Flood. But, if you could have looked at the street corners and under the trees of the villages at the bottom of the now-peaceful waters, you would have seen a glittering substance starting to crystallize. Probably around the invisible core of the supersaturated liquid people.

The Stick

It was a muggy Sunday in June . . .

On the crowded roof of the department store across from the station, supervising my two kids, I looked down at the avenue swollen with cars and people after the rain.

Spotting an opening, just vacated, between the ventilator and the stairs, I quickly wedged myself into it. I lifted each of the children in turn so they could see over the railing. They soon got tired of this, but now I was interested. It was nothing unusual, I thought. Actually, there were more adults clinging to the rail than children. Most of the children, quickly getting bored, started badgering their parents to go home. The adults, though, scolding them as if they'd interrupted their work, dreamily nestled their chins on their forearms on the railing again.

Of course, it may have been a slightly guilty pleasure. Even so, it wasn't anything to particularly call into question. I was simply in an absentminded mood. Or at least I was not thinking of anything that later on I would have to try to remember. Only—perhaps it was the humid air—I grew curiously irritable and lost my temper with the kids.

The oldest, as if he were angry at me, was yelling "Daddy!" Without thinking, as if to escape his voice, I leaned way out over the railing. It was just a momentary impulse, nothing dangerous. But all of a sudden my body was floating in air. The voice yelling "Daddy!" still in my ears, I started falling.

I don't know if it was while falling that it happened, or if it happened, and then I fell, but when I came to, still falling, I'd turned into a stick. Not thick, not slender—I was a straight, handy stick about three feet long. The voice yelled "Daddy!" again. An opening appeared in the quickly moving crowd on the pavement below. Aiming at it, turning end over end, I fell faster and faster. Bouncing off the pavement with a sharp, dry sound, I hit a tree and lodged in a crack in the gutter between the sidewalk and the trolley tracks. Along the railing above, the pale little faces of my children were neatly lined up side by side.

The passersby glared angrily up at the roof. The doorman standing guard at the entrance, saying he would really get those brats for this, sprinted up the stairs. Excitedly, people shook their fists and made threats. Because of that, I stayed where I was in the gutter unnoticed by anyone for a while.

Finally a student noticed me. He was with two companions. One was a student like himself, dressed in the same uniform, and the other seemed to be their teacher. The two students, in stature, expression, and way of wearing their hats, were as alike as twins. The teacher, with a white mustache and powerful spectacles, was a very serene, tall gentleman.

Pulling me free, the first student said in a somehow regretful tone:

"Even this kind of thing, when it's no longer any use, has to perish."

"Let me have it," the teacher said with a smile. Receiving me from the student, he shook me two or three times, then said: "It's lighter than I thought. But nobody wants it for anything. Such as it is, though, it's a good object of study for you two. Perhaps just the thing for your first practical exercise. Let's think a little, shall we, of what can be learned from this stick."

Using me as a walking stick, the old gentleman started walking.

The two students followed behind. Avoiding the crowd, they came out into the square in front of the station and looked around for a bench. The benches all being taken, though, they sat down side by side on the edge of the grass. Holding me up in both hands, the teacher narrowed his eyes as he scrutinized me against the light. Just then, I noticed a strange thing. Apparently noticing it at the same moment, the students said almost in unison: "Teacher, your mustache . . ." It seemed to be a false mustache. The left end had come unstuck and was flapping in the breeze. The teacher, calmly nodding agreement, pressed the mustache back in place with a saliva-moistened fingertip. As if nothing had happened, he turned to the students on either side of him and spoke.

"Now, what sort of things can you infer from this stick? Try analyzing it, judging it, and deciding on its punishment."

First, the student on the right took me and looked at me from various angles. "The first thing one notices is that this stick has an upper and a lower part." Sliding me through his hand closed in a tube, he continued: "The upper part is fairly ingrained with grime. The lower part is rather worn and abraded. This means, I take it, that this stick was not merely thrown away by the roadside but was used by people for some specific purpose. However, this stick was subjected to pretty hard use. There are nicks and scratches all over it. Furthermore, doesn't the fact that it was used for a long time without being thrown away mean that this stick, during its lifetime, was a simple, honest tool?"

"What you say is correct. But it's a little too sentimental," the teacher said, a smile in his voice.

Whereupon, whether it was to refute those words or not, the student on the left said, in a tone almost harsh:

"I think that this stick was probably completely useless. It's much *too* simple, isn't it? It's degrading for a human being to use a mere stick as a tool. Even a monkey can use a stick."

"But, to state the reverse," the student on the right rejoined, "cannot one say that the stick is the origin of all tools? What's more, without being especially altered, its uses are many. It can guide the blind man and train the dog. As a lever, it can move heavy objects, and it can thrash an adversary."

"The stick guides the blind man? I am unable to agree with that opinion. It's not the case that the blind man is guided by the stick. I believe that, using the stick, he guides himself."

"Well, isn't that to say that this was an honest stick?"

"Perhaps so. However, if Teacher is able to thrash me with this stick, I am also able to thrash Teacher with it."

Finally the teacher burst out laughing. "It's a real pleasure listening to you two argue. You're as alike as a pair of melons. However, you are simply saying the same thing in different ways. To summarize your statements, this man was a stick. That, for the necessity of referring to this man, is an adequate answer . . . In brief, this stick was a stick."

"But . . ." the student on the right said, a lingering regret in his voice. "To say that it was able to be a stick, don't we have to recognize its special characteristics? I have seen all sorts of human beings in our specimen room, but I've never once seen a stick. This kind of simple honesty is unusual, after all . . ."

"No, no. Just because it's not in our specimen room doesn't mean it's unusual," the teacher replied. "On the contrary, it's all too commonplace. In short, it's absolutely banal, and therefore we do not recognize any necessity to deliberately pick it up and examine it."

The students, simultaneously, as if they'd agreed on it, raised their faces and looked at the crowd around them. The teacher smiled. "No, it's not the case that all these people are sticks. When I say that being a stick is excessively ordinary, I speak in the qualitative rather than the quantitative sense. It's the same thing as mathematicians not saying much about the properties of a triangle. Because there are no new discoveries to be made from it." Pausing, he added: "By the way, what punishment do you two intend to hand down?"

"Do we have to inflict a punishment even on this stick?" the student on the right asked, as if in a quandary.

"What do you think?" The teacher turned to the student on the left.

"Of course we must punish it. To punish the dead is our raison d'être. We exist, therefore we must punish."

"Well, then, what is the appropriate punishment?"

The two students each thought hard for a while. The teacher, taking me, idly began drawing something in the dirt. It was a diagram without any abstract meaning. It soon sprouted arms and legs and became the figure of a monster. Then he began erasing the picture. When he'd finished, he stood up and, gazing into the distance, he muttered:

"Even you two must have thought long enough by now. The answer is so difficult because it's too simple. Surely you remember it from one of my lectures . . . Those who are judged by not being judged . . ."

"I remember," both students said at once. "It's enough for courts on earth to judge a certain percentage of the population. But we, until there are immortal human beings, have to judge them all. Compared to the number of people, however, we are extremely few. If we had to judge all the dead in the same way, we would probably work ourselves to death. Fortunately, there exists this convenient category of people whom we judge by not judging . . ."

"This stick is a representative example of that category." Smiling, the teacher let go of me. I fell down, and started to roll away. Stopping me with the tip of his shoe, the teacher said: "Therefore, the best punishment is to leave it behind like this. Most likely someone will pick it up and, just as during its lifetime, use it as a stick in various ways."

One of the students, as if it had just occurred to him, said: "What would this stick have thought if it could have heard us?"

The teacher looked at the student as if pitying him, but said nothing. Then, urging the two, he started walking. The students, seemingly worried about me, turned around and looked back at me several times. Soon, however, they were swallowed up by the crowd and disappeared. Somebody stepped on me. I was pressed halfway into the rain-softened dirt.

"Daddy, Daddy, Daddy . . ." I heard voices calling. They sounded like my children, and they didn't sound like my children. It would not be strange if, among the thousands of children in this crowd, there were many others who had to call out their father's name.

Notes on the Authors

SHIGA NAOYA [1883–1971] has been called the "god" of the Japanese short story. "The Razor," in which an unsuspecting customer has his throat cut by a barber irritated by his vulgarity, according to the critic Ara Masahito, "expresses to perfection the persecution complex that everyone feels in a barber shop." "At Kinosaki" is the story of the author-narrator recuperating at a hot springs inn after a near-fatal accident. While there, he witnesses three little deaths—of a wasp, a rat with a skewer through its throat trying to swim across a stream while being stoned by villagers, and a lizard whose death the author inadvertently causes when he hits it with a stone tossed to make it go into the water—whose ascending scale of epiphany brings his own brush with death into proper perspective.

OZAKI SHIRO [1897–1964] was born in the Hazu district of Aichi Prefecture. "River Deer" and "The Wagtail's Nest," both written in 1927, are probably based on the author's experience and observation while staying at a hot springs inn in Izu. The critic Takahashi Yoshitaka comments that these excellent stories established Ozaki as a writer. He continues: "Human relationships and wild creatures—the river frogs and the wagtail—find an echo in each other like that

175

of linked verses. Furthermore, one is not outweighed or explained away by the other. Each is itself, and a symbol of the other, in a creative synthesis deep in hidden meaning and charm. If a less talented writer had attempted this theme, it would probably have left a bad taste of sentimentality. But in these two stories, there is none of that. We cannot but be astonished by the peerless clarity with which the wagtail and the river deer are shown to have a profound connection with the most human part of ourselves."

YASUNARI KAWABATA [1899–1972], Japan's Nobel Prize winner, was born in 1899 in Osaka. His father died when he was one, and his mother when he was two. The three stories in this collection are taken from *Thumbprint Novels* (*Tanagokoro no Shosetsu*, literally "Palm of the Hand Stories"), his early major work. Edward Seidensticker comments: "The expression might be translated as 'vest-pocket stories,' and the form, which to my knowledge no one else has made such considerable use of, might be called the prose equivalent of haiku." In these tiny short stories, Kawabata's grand themes of loneliness and disillusion are sometimes conspicuously absent, as in "The Grasshopper and the Bell Cricket," "The Silverberry Thief," and "The Young Lady of Suruga," or perhaps it would be better to say are sweetly attenuated.

After an early life of great poverty, SHIMAKI KENSAKU [1903–1945] began in 1934 to publish many books, of which *In Search of Life*, a novel about struggling farmers, may be the most representative. Shimaki died of tuberculosis two days after the close of World War II. He has written of himself: "There is no chance of my being a great writer, or even a strong or particularly acute writer. What I would wish for myself, however weak or minor this may be, is a work in which there is something clear and straightforward. As if one stood in a field and, turning around, saw a narrow road that ran straight and true at the far edge of that field." "The Red Frog" was Shimaki's last work.

HAYASHI FUMIKO [1904–1951] wrote of herself, in "Diary of a Wanderer": "I am by fate a wanderer. I have no native place. My father was a man of Iyo in Shikoku, an itinerant peddler of dry goods. My mother was a maid at a hot springs inn in Sakurajima of Kyushu. Since she had married an outlander, she was driven out of her hometown. The couple came to rest in a place called Shimonoseki in Yamaguchi Prefecture. That Shimonoseki is where I was born." There is a roadside shrine to her outside the inn where her mother worked. A local tourist bus stops there regularly, and the girl guide sings a song from Hayashi's work, a song about love of family and home. On the literary marker, this poem by Hayashi is engraved:

> Hana no inochi wa mijikakute
> Nigashiki koto nomi ookariki
>
> (The life of a flower is short
> Only bitter things are many)

DAZAI OSAMU [1909–1948] was born in Aomori in northeastern Japan. He has written: "I have written my suicide note. It is 'Memories.' At present, these 'Memories' are what is called my maiden literary work. I thought I would like to give an unadorned account of the evil I suffered in my childhood . . . I wrote the piece in the autumn of my twenty-fourth year. Sitting in my one-room detached quarters, looking out on a wide, deserted garden rankly overgrown with weeds, I lost my ability to smile. I felt as if I had died the second death." Dazai meant what he said literally. "Memories" started out as a suicide note, the confession of "a dirty child" which, by the anxiety it caused him, "kindled a faint light in my emptiness," that of literary aspiration, a desire to make it better. Dazai's work is much loved by the young. His grave (he finally did commit suicide in his thirty-ninth year by throwing himself into the Tamagawa Reservoir with his mistress) is decorated with flowers by Tokyo schoolgirls on each anniversary of his death.

KOBO ABÉ [1924–   ] is regarded as the most distinctively peculiar of the postwar writers. His work goes completely against the dominant realistic mode of twentieth-century Japanese literature. He is, in fact, a literary surrealist, Kafka being his major detectable influence. What has made his work acceptable to the older generation of writers is its fine literary quality. "The Red Cocoon," one of his earliest stories, won an important literary prize. In his best work, strange, evocative images give his stories depth and resonance.

Other Titles in Tuttle Library of Japanese Literature

BOTCHAN *by Sōseki Natsume; translated by Umeji Sasaki*

> "*Botchan* is one of the most widely-read novels in modern Japan. . . . It superbly delineates, through the sentiments and actions of the turn-of-the-century hero, inimitable characteristics of an old Japan."
>
> —*The Oriental Economist*

THE MAKIOKA SISTERS *by Junichirō Tanizaki; translated by Edward G. Seidensticker*

> "A genuine masterpiece."
>
> —*Yale Review*

THE SEA AND POISON *by Shūsaku Endō; translated by Michael Gallagher*

> "A picture of Japan in transition—tangible, sharp as the opening of a Hemingway short story."
>
> —*The Guardian*

THE SETTING SUN *by Osamu Dazai; translated by Donald Keene*

> "Dazai's masterpiece is generally considered to be the novel *Setting Sun* . . . which in fine, sensitive prose describes the final disintegration of an aristocratic family in postwar Japan."
>
> —Ivan Morris

THE OLD CAPITAL *by Yasunari Kawabata; translated by J. Martin Holman*

"*The Old Capital* is suffused with nostalgia for traditional culture; the descriptions of gardens, ceremonies, costumes, and crafts are tender and precise, as lyrical and resonant as a haiku."

—*Vogue*

THE RUINED MAP *by Kobo Abé; translated by E. Dale Saunders*

"*The Ruined Map* is one of the rare Japanese works of avant-garde fiction, and it shows a craftsmanship that has few peers."

—Donald Keene

SOME PREFER NETTLES *by Junichirō Tanizaki; translated by Edward G. Seidensticker*

"A fascinating novel which gives an intimate picture of the dilemma of a Japanese family torn between the attractions of modern Westernized life and the strong pull of Japanese tradition."

—George B. Sansom

PALM-OF-THE-HAND STORIES *by Yasunari Kawabata; translated by Lane Dunlop and J. Martin Holman*

"The icy-fine configurations of these deceptively delicate dramas reveal characters beset by loneliness, impotence and a longing for the past almost too intense to be borne. . . . Lovingly translated from the Japanese: dark gems, tantalizing, sometimes baffling—and special."

—*Kirkus Reviews*